NGAU grüßt
Marlboro
HONDA
Marlboro
12
Shell
Shell

AYRTON SENNA
PORTRAIT OF A CHAMPION

By ALAN HENRY

HAZLETON PUBLISHING

PUBLISHER
Richard Poulter

EXECUTIVE PUBLISHER
Elizabeth Le Breton

ART EDITOR
Steve Small

PRODUCTION CONTROLLER
Peter Lovering

PRODUCTION ASSISTANT
Wendy Owen

STATISTICS
John Taylor

Colour photography by:

Front and back cover	–	Keith Sutton
Pages 49-57	–	Keith Sutton
Page 58	–	Nigel Snowdon
Pages 59-64	–	Keith Sutton

Black and white photographs contributed by:
Diana Burnett, Nigel Snowdon and Keith Sutton.

The author would like to thank Motor Racing Publications for permission to quote from Doug Nye's *Theme Lotus*.

This first edition published in 1988 by
Hazleton Publishing, 3 Richmond Hill, Richmond,
Surrey TW10 6RE.

ISBN: 0-905138-60-0

Printed by BAS Printers Ltd, Over Wallop, Hampshire.

Typesetting by First Impression Type Ltd, Richmond, Surrey.

DISTRIBUTORS

UK & OTHER MARKETS
Osprey Publishing Limited, 59 Grosvenor Street,
London W1X 9DA

USA
Motorbooks International,
PO Box 2, 729 Prospect Ave.,
Osceola, Wisconsin 54020

AUSTRALIA
Technical Book & Magazine Co. Pty,
289-299 Swanston Street, Melbourne, Victoria 3000

NEW ZEALAND
David Bateman Ltd,
PO Box 65062, Mairangi Bay,
Auckland 10

Marlboro
Shell
BOSS
MEN'S FASHION

Senna takes the chequered flag and victory in the Japanese Grand Prix to become the 1988 World Champion.

Sunday, 30 October 1988. The day dawns brightly, but temperatures are kept down by a biting wind. The grandstands and spectator enclosures at Suzuka have been packed from an early hour, the mad-keen Japanese enthusiasts having camped out, in neatly disciplined lines leading up to the turnstiles, since the previous sunset. They have come to see a World Championship decided.

In the McLaren garage, the atmosphere is tense. Throughout the year, up to this point, it has varied between the relaxed and the highly charged, depending on how changing circumstances have subtly altered the relationship between McLaren's two driving stars, who have turned the 1988 Formula One World Championship into their own personal playground.

Now Alain Prost and Ayrton Senna realise that the showdown could be at hand. Mathematically, only the Brazilian is able to clinch the title on this particular day. Prost, fighting against the odds, can only hope to carry the battle on to the final round in Adelaide, a fortnight hence – and to do that he must win here in Japan, unless a driver from a rival team can keep his team-mate away from first place.

The Frenchman's qualifying sessions haven't been without problem, and he had an upset stomach to contend with on the first day, but he's in a confident mood. He would have been in pole position, he thinks, except for a missed gearchange. That privilege, however, is reserved for Ayrton Senna, the 12th occasion on which he has started from the number one slot in the 15 races so far this year.

Race morning is rife with speculation. Can Senna win his record eighth victory of the year? Is it possible that Prost can repeat his Estoril and Jerez performances, where he trounced his team-mate convincingly? Eventually the two McLarens lead the field away on the pre-race parade lap. It's the 11th time in 1988 they have monopolised the front row of the grid.

As the starting light blinks green, Prost is presented with a

Opposite: *Ayrton on the rotrum at Suzuka.*

once-in-a-lifetime bonus: Senna jerks forward and stalls – 'a combination of my mistake and an over-sensitive clutch pedal'. Gerhard Berger fishtails past the Brazilian's near-stationary MP4/4 to the left, Nelson Piquet goes to the right. But, aided by the Suzuka startline, which is on a downhill slope, Ayrton has just enough momentum to bump the McLaren into life. The Honda V6 stalls on him again! By the time he coaxes it back onto full song, Prost is leading into the first right-hander ahead of Berger's Ferrari and Ivan Capelli's March.

First time round, Prost is comfortably ahead. He has covered the 3.641-mile lap from a standing start in 1m 55.293s. Senna, now in eighth place, has taken 2m 04.246s. He is nine seconds behind and has the Ferraris of Berger and Michele Alboreto, the Benettons of Thierry Boutsen and Alessandro Nannini, plus Riccardo Patrese's Williams, between him and Prost. It's over. You don't give Alain Prost that sort of advantage and not live to regret it. The battle for the title will go all the way to Adelaide …

Berger is tight on Prost's tail for the first couple of laps, but the Ferrari is no measure for the McLaren-Honda in terms of fuel consumption. By lap four, the Austrian's challenge has faded. On lap six, Capelli's March goes winging by into second place, the Italian bent on challenging the leading McLaren. Even though Senna is seventh on lap two, sixth on lap three, he doesn't seem to be making up significant ground on his team-mate. Estoril and Jerez all over again, say the Prost fans.

Capelli, however, has other ideas. The McLaren duo may think their two-horse race for the title is of paramount importance, but the little Italian is out to upset the applecart. He's already been second to Prost at Estoril, where the Frenchman freely conceded that Ivan had kept him on his toes. Now, in front of all the guests brought along by Leyton House, the March team's Japanese sponsor, Capelli is out to prove once more that he's got what it takes. On lap nine he's only 3.6 sec-

onds behind the leading McLaren. Five laps later he is less than a second adrift when Suzuka is brushed by a light rain shower. By now Senna is third.

Prost really isn't too keen on the rain and sustains a pace which is just sufficient to retain the lead – but Capelli is close enough to capitalise on any slight hiccup. Coming through the tight chicane before the pits, at the end of lap 16, Prost hesitates momentarily as Aguri Suzuki, the Japanese novice standing in for an unwell Yannick Dalmas in the second LC Lola, pirouettes to a temporary standstill.

Capelli goes for it. Aiming his March down the outside of the McLaren, he draws level as they approach the startline and just noses ahead, tripping the timing beam fractionally before 'Mr Prost', as he deferentially refers to the twice World Champion. He is leading a Grand Prix for the first time in his short career, but the naturally aspirated car just hasn't got the power to cut in front of Prost. Alain eases back ahead as they lean into the next right-hander.

By now Senna is gobbling up their advantage and, three laps

later, the Brazilian is presented with second place when the March falters with an electrical problem. Capelli's challenge is spent. So it is business as usual, 1988 style, with a McLaren-Honda 1-2 at the head of the field.

Prost is experiencing the first signs of gearbox trouble, missing the odd shift here and there. He seems to be holding his rival at bay – but only just. At the end of lap 27 the Frenchman is slowed by the troublesome Rial of Andrea de Cesaris, at the same tight chicane before the pits. Senna seizes his opportunity and, with an overwhelmingly inevitable surge, slips alongside Prost as they race for the right-hander after the pits and then slices through into the lead. Alain gives him precisely enough room, not a millimetre more. That's all Ayrton Senna needs.

Cutting a path through slower traffic is one of the Brazilian driver's great talents, but the back-markers are more than usually unhelpful at Suzuka on this dank, overcast afternoon. Initially Senna pulls away from Prost, building up a five-second advantage. Then Alain goes on the counter-attack, but his challenge is defeated by some appalling baulking, notably by Satoru Nakajima who, with a conspicuous lack of consideration, holds up both McLarens with his Lotus. And with five laps to go it begins to rain again, so badly that Senna can be seen signalling to the officials that they ought to think about flagging the race.

The officials take no notice, so Senna runs the full 51-lap distance to take the chequered flag just over 13 seconds ahead of the other McLaren. It is his eighth victory of the 1988 season, an all-time record for wins in a single year. The previous record of seven wins had been established by the late Jim Clark, at the wheel of a Lotus-Coventry Climax, as long ago as 1963, and another 21 years passed before Alain Prost matched that. Now Ayrton Senna has beaten the record – and joined Emerson Fittipaldi and Nelson Piquet as the third Brazilian to win the World Championship for Drivers.

Mission Accomplished.

Another winner's garland to round off Ayrton's FF2000 season; there would be more waiting in F3 the following year.

There was something about Ayrton Senna's whole demeanour that marked him as an unusually confident and out-of-the-ordinary racer when he turned up at Silverstone in late 1983. The occasion was a Marlboro-sponsored F1 test of a McLaren MP4/1C, the Brazilian's reward for pipping Martin Brundle to the 1983 British F3 title.

Here was a young man who didn't conform to any stereotypes. He wasn't over-awed and, if he was nervous, then he wasn't

Right: *Clean pair of heels. Well ahead of the somewhat frenetic FF1600 opposition, exiting the Woodcote chicane at Silverstone.*

Dominant form: rounding Lodge Corner (below right), *Oulton Park, during his FF1600 campaign.*

about to show it. He'd already had a test drive of one of Frank Williams's cars earlier in the season, hurling Keke Rosberg's FW08C round Donington Park with a wheel-locking abandon that made it clear he'd been born to handle a Grand Prix car. Senna was formally cordial to the small clutch of press men who'd turned out to watch him drive the McLaren, but there was no trace of servility about him. If anything, he seemed rather a cold fish, private and extremely intense. Self-doubt clearly played no part in his make-up.

Most youngsters would have been extremely circumspect in such a situation, but Ayrton Senna took Ron Dennis's breath away – although the McLaren boss might be loth to admit it today. Instead of backing off when he felt the McLaren's Cosworth DFV engine begin to lose its edge, the Brazilian kept his foot down hard all the way to the end of a really quick lap. And the car blew up, quite comprehensively, a matter of yards after crossing the timing line. It is not recorded whether Senna apologised for this mechanical mayhem, but he certainly wasn't going to be forgotten.

Born on 21 March 1960, the son of wealthy São Paulo businessman, Milton da Silva, Ayrton grew up in a secure and comfortable family environment. To this day, he values and fiercely protects the privacy and sense of belonging his upbringing imbued in him. He adores both his family and his native Brazil, speaking of them with respectful affection. To say he was born with a silver spoon in his mouth may be going too far: his father certainly had the wherewithal to insulate him from life's harsher realities, so in that respect he was fortunate, and seems to appreciate it, but he was clearly disciplined well as a child.

Karting provided him with his basic grounding in motor sport. In fact, his father built him a kart when he was only four years old. Later, da Silva Senior disciplined his son with the sanction that if his monthly school reports fell short of the mark, there was no karting for a month. It must have been a

Highly tuned delivery.
chains
Mobil Mobil Mobil
Mobil Mobil

painful penalty for the schoolboy enthusiast.

When Ayrton Senna da Silva exploded onto the British national Formula Ford scene in 1981, most observers simply saw yet another unusually talented Brazilian following in the footsteps of several celebrated countrymen. But, as is often the case, there was a lot more hard racing experience underpinning his efforts than one might have suspected. By then he had been kart racing for eight years, having made his debut in July 1973.

Starting in the 100 cc category, where he remained for his first few years of racing, he then decided to have a crack at the World Championship. Held at Le Mans in 1977, and at Estoril two years later, young Senna da Silva contested both of these one-race shoot-outs. He managed sixth in the former event and finished runner-up to Dutchman Peter Koene in 1979 having been defeated, in effect, by the complexities of the aggregate scoring system which placed a premium on the best two results out of the three finals. He was second again in 1980, the championship contested this time at Belgium's Nivelles circuit. The following season he was up and running in Formula Ford.

For 1981 he beat a path to Ralph Firman's door and fixed himself up with a Van Diemen FF1600 machine. Firman recalls him as being unusually determined, but John Kirkpatrick, long-time manager of the Jim Russell Racing Drivers' School – now at Donington Park, but then at Snetterton – remembers him as a very quiet and totally unobtrusive youngster. 'If a group of us went down to the pub, he would come along, but he would just stand quietly to one side, sipping his drink, and only seemed to speak when spoken to. He was really very shy.'

Ayrton won his third race, setting the tone for the year. By the end of the season he had taken the chequered flag 12 times in 20 races, clinching both the RAC and Townsend Thoresen titles. But the Brazilian finished the year in a somewhat confused state of mind, disillusioned that advancement even from

A fresh-faced youngster, new to FF1600, in 1981.

LONGINES
11

RUSHEN GREEN RACING
AYRTON SENNA
11

Left: *One of Ayrton's most memorable victories was at the Osterreichring, where his Van Diemen led from start to finish under the watchful eye of the Grand Prix team-managers.*

With his young wife, Liliane (centre left), *in 1981. Their marriage fell victim to the intensity of Senna's motor racing ambition.*

Bottom left: *A tight line through the Mallory Park hairpin on his way to victory in the British-based Pace Petroleum series.*

this lowly level depended every bit as much on the financial resources available as on sheer talent. It was a conundrum which he couldn't fully understand – and it annoyed him. Moreover, life in rural Norfolk had taken its toll on his marriage to Liliane, his childhood sweetheart. He returned to Brazil that winter and almost turned his back on motor racing for good. There was talk of his going into the family business, learning about cattle in order to help his father manage their huge Brazilian ranch in Goiania. Eventually, however, he came to terms with the vagaries of racing, raised the finance and returned to England for the 1982 season. Alone. 'I just couldn't resist the attraction of a steering wheel and a racing car,' he reflected in 1988. 'Up to that point I had raced largely for fun and, if I had not come back to England, I would probably have continued racing, just as a hobby, in Brazil.'

He had hoped to graduate to F3 but the budget was not available, so he opted to run a semi-works Van Diemen in Formula Ford 2000, entered by Rushen Green Racing. His blitz on both the British and European series made his FF1600 exploits pale into absolute insignificance. This time he won 21 out of the 27 races in which he took part, including triumphs in front of the F1 fraternity at Zolder, Hockenheim and the Osterreichring. People were undoubtedly impressed, but there was definitely an underlying feeling that FF2000 couldn't be exactly the most competitive of arenas if this young Brazilian could produce this level of domination. Wait until he gets to F3, said the doubters, then it will be different.

It wasn't. At the end of the year he arranged a drive in a West Surrey Racing Ralt at the televised Thruxton meeting. Starting from pole, he won handsomely. To some extent the outing could be regarded as an opportunity for some mutual assessment between the two parties, prior to finalising a deal for a full-scale assault on the British F3 Championship the following year.

That series polarised into a battle between Ayrton (who for

Left: *Ayrton with his mother, Neyde.*

Below: *The drudge of international travel – no Learjet in those early days!*

Bottom: *Relaxed and cheerful, a picture of informality.*

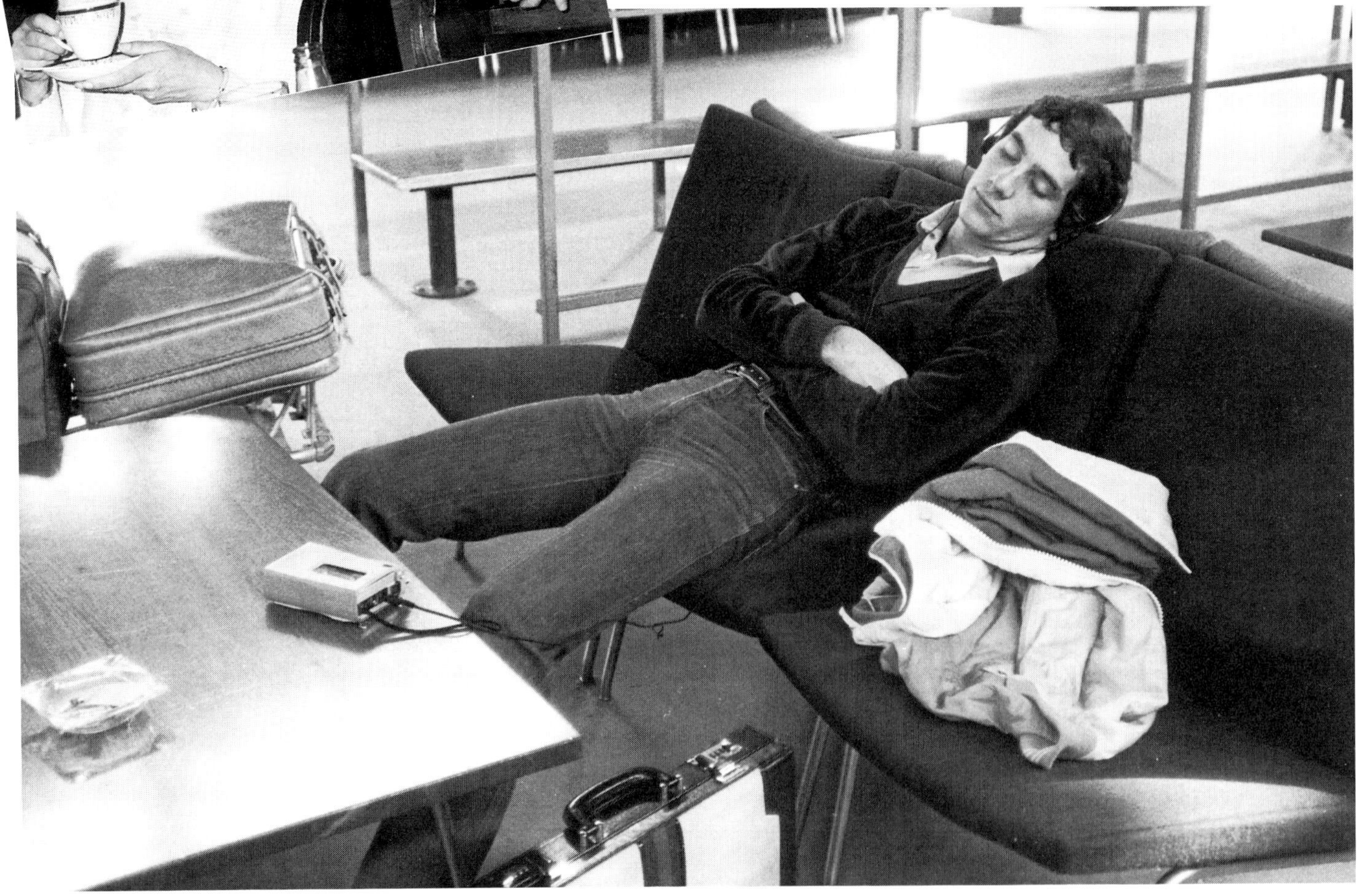

Left: *Off-duty, enjoying a relaxing meal, suitably casual...*

Below: *Ayrton celebrates as he clinches the FF2000 championship with victory here at Jyllandsring.*

Right: *No patches! A few years later there would be no shortage of multi-million-dollar sponsorship decals dripping from the Brazilian's racing overalls.*

racing purposes had dropped his paternal family surname, preferring to be known simply by his mother's family name, Senna – just as Nelson Piquet Sauto-Maior had done some years earlier) and British rising star, Martin Brundle. In a season punctuated by several spectacular shunts, a by-product of Ayrton's absolute refusal to accept second best, the Brazilian pipped his English rival at the very last race, and took the British title. Finally, to round off the year, he won superbly at Macau. Unsurprisingly, Ayrton remains unshakably convinced of the value of F3 as an international training ground. He firmly rejects the notion that this junior category is hamstrung by lack of power and too much grip. 'No, no ... it teaches you discipline, experience, how to behave from a technical point of view. It teaches you how to drive with economy of effort.'

Above: *The instrument of success: Senna's West Surrey Racing Ralt RT3 carried the Brazilian to the 1983 Marlboro British F3 title.*

Right: *On the verge of the big time! Senna clasps his hands together with delight as he samples the fruits of F3 victory. His entrant, Dick Bennetts, is on the left.*

Below: *Showering the champagne with uninhibited delight.*

Brundle and Senna together in '83, both destined for F1 the following year.

Above right: *Side by side, running for the first corner at Thruxton.*

Right: *The ferocity of his F3 title duel with Martin Brundle revealed the strength of Senna's resolve and his unwillingness to settle for second place. Here Ayrton* (left) *and Brundle survey the tangled wreckage of their interlocked Ralts at Cadwell Park.*

Jeans
Pool
Marlboro F3
CADERNETA DE POUPANCA
1
BANERJ
CHAMPION
RACING
for BRITAIN
Sieger
GAS DETECTION
2
Marlboro F3

BANERJ
Marlboro F3
AYRTON
SENNA
Jeans
Pool
1
2

Right: *First F1 test. Ayrton samples a Williams FW08C at Donington Park, summer 1983.*

Below right: *Portent for the future: in the cockpit of the McLaren MP4/1C at Silverstone. Senna blew up its engine, but Ron Dennis has now clearly forgiven this transgression!*

But there was much more to Ayrton Senna than simply an ability to win motor races. As Frank Williams, who presided over that maiden F1 test at Donington, was quick to realise, this Brazilian was unusually intelligent and articulate. He could describe how the car was behaving in lucid, graphic detail. It was the continuation of a trait first noticed by Dennis Rushen and Robin Green in Ayrton's FF2000 Van Diemen days. Senna had a rare gift: the capacity to slow the whole car performance process down in his mind – and this ability was linked to an uncanny sensitivity when it came to assessing how quickly it might be possible to lap. Only occasionally would his Latin temperament bubble through to the surface and cause him to do something slightly unpredictable.

By the time Senna was winning at Macau in Bennetts' F3 Ralt, the die had been cast for his F1 career. Already there were people queuing up for the services of this remarkably committed new boy. Bernie Ecclestone was keen to have him alongside Nelson Piquet and, indeed, at the 1983 British Grand Prix the elder Brazilian spent a long time chatting to the new star. Senna was later to say that Piquet had indicated he would not object if he joined the team. However, much as Bernie wanted that to happen, constraints imposed by various sponsorship agreements blocked it. 'I don't know whether Nelson also eventually said no,' Ayrton later reflected, 'but if he did, I can't say I would have blamed him...'

Eventually Ayrton decided to go to Toleman – ironically, as it turned out later, as successor to the Renault-bound Derek Warwick – but not before Peter Warr had tried energetically to recruit the Brazilian rising star into the Team Lotus fold. However, Imperial Tobacco had been keen to retain Nigel Mansell and Senna, showing shrewd judgement, preferred to make his Grand Prix debut with a less celebrated team, keeping the pressure on himself to a minimum as he learnt the ropes. It was not a process that would take him very long.

Toleman team-chief Alex Hawkridge quickly realised the

TAG
DENIM
Mobil
GOODYEAR
Save the Children
saudia
CHAMPION

Marlboro
UNIPART
HERCULES
MICHELIN
7

long-term quality of their new recruit. He was also impressed, and sometimes a little indignant, with Ayrton's forthright approach. 'No matter what the situation, he always, without exception, felt that he was right,' reflected Hawkridge, 'and what made it even more infuriating at times was that he was generally correct. His capacity to control and channel his emotions was also remarkable. But he could be two distinct personalities. Watching the painstaking manner in which he scrutinised his contract with us, that meticulous attention to detail, contrasted with his off-duty character – socially, he could become schoolboyish, almost giggly.'

Yet, even at this early stage of his career, one was aware that the unduly intelligent Brazilian was someone special. Over the next four seasons he was to develop into a man so totally absorbed by every detail of his work – his obsession – that only a few people, working alongside him, with his team, can make contact with him. He radiates such an all-pervading feeling of intense concentration that one gets the impression he is attempting to probe every inner technical facet of his car's make-up. This sort of approach leaves no room for the frivolous. Talking to Senna involves shifting up a gear mentally. Small talk isn't to his taste, but ask a very specific and detailed question and he will respond in correspondingly painstaking vein. He doesn't deal in 'ifs' and 'maybes'.

None of his answers is superficial, and although English is a foreign language to him, the way in which he has mastered it stands as an acute embarrassment to those of us who, at best, can only mumble the odd few phrases in tourist French. Talking to him prior to the 1988 Portuguese Grand Prix, we touched on the subject of a test session he had carried out with the new Honda V10-engined prototype at the tiny Pembrey track in South Wales. 'Down the M4, just beyond Port Talbot, isn't it?' I enquired. 'Near *Llanelli*, actually,' he explained. It stopped me in my tracks. Richard Burton couldn't have pronounced 'Llanelli' more accurately...

MAGIRUS
Segafredo
MAGIRUS
CAMPARI
27
GOODYEAR

Second F1 race, first championship point. Ayrton rounds Kyalami's Clubhouse Corner ahead of Michele Alboreto's Ferrari during the 1984 South African Grand Prix. His Toleman TG183B lost its nose cone, but the Brazilian battled home to finish an exhausted sixth.

Senna's talent was such that it quickly outgrew what Toleman could offer him. The team began 1983 with the Hart-engined TG183B and Ayrton scored his first World Championship point at Kyalami, the second race on the calendar. But it was clear that Pirelli's rubber was simply not on the same competitive level as the contemporary Michelins, so after a truncated and unsatisfactory weekend at Imola, which saw Senna failing to qualify for the San Marino Grand Prix, a switch to the French rubber was engineered in time for the French Grand Prix at Dijon-Prenois. Both Ayrton and team-mate Johnny Cecotto retired their brand new TG184s with turbo failure – but next on the race calendar was Monaco, where Ayrton was destined to put his name up in lights.

Ayrton qualified 13th and lined up with his colleagues on a rain-soaked starting grid for one of the wettest races in Monaco history. Splashing through the murk, he steadily picked up the pace and began to work his way through the pack, looking for all the world as though he had been driving F1 cars in such dire conditions all his life.

By lap 16 he was up to third, and had Niki Lauda's McLaren firmly in his sights. It only took him another three laps to overtake the Austrian twice World Champion, after which he set off purposefully after Prost. Coming up to the 30-lap mark the rain intensified; Ayrton had moved to within seven seconds of the McLaren, surviving a hair-raising incident when he glanced the chicane kerb, briefly two-wheeling his TG184, but retaining control. By now Prost was signalling skywards that Clerk of the Course, Jacky Ickx, should stop the race as the track was virtually flooded.

On lap 33, Ickx obliged and Prost pulled over to the right as he saw the chequered flag, allowing Senna to burst past on a cloud of spume and cross the line first. Ayrton thought he had won! He later felt cheated – as did the rest of the Toleman team – when everybody realised that in such circumstances the race order is taken on the lap *prior* to the chequered flag. Half points

Opposite: *Glory day: the Michelin-shod Toleman TG184, rocketing through the spray at Monaco to second place, hard on Prost's tail, in a half-points finish.*

were awarded for this event – but Senna had made his mark.

Wet-weather form has always been one of the crucial indices by which one judges great racing drivers and Ayrton Senna certainly stands up to scrutiny in this respect. In fact, when one analyses his career performance over the years, wet-weather brilliance has been one of the basic cornerstones of his success. In 1985, he was to win his first Grand Prix, in a Lotus-Renault 97T at Estoril, in conditions so appalling that Alain Prost's McLaren spun out of the race on the start/finish straight. Three years later this same skill would win him the British Grand Prix at Silverstone and the German Grand Prix at Hockenheim, both giant strides towards his World Championship title. Bearing this capability in mind, there was something peculiarly ironic about the way in which Senna drove the last few laps of his title-clincher, the 1988 Japanese Grand Prix, pointing anxiously skywards to indicate to race officials (in an ironic echo of Prost at Monaco in 1984) that another light shower was brushing Suzuka and that perhaps they ought to think about flagging the race early. But then, of course, they were all on slicks on this occasion...

Throughout the summer of 1984 Senna consolidated his reputation. Third place at Brands Hatch behind Lauda's McLaren and Warwick's Renault proved to be another significant feather in his cap, and there were already rumblings of interest in his services from other teams, notably Lotus. Peter Warr was extremely anxious to secure the services of the man he was later to describe as 'in my experience the most complete driver since Jimmy Clark'. He convinced his sponsors that Senna was the man and duly signed him just prior to the 1984 Dutch Grand Prix.

Much has been written on the subject of Senna's departure from Toleman. He did, indeed, have a buy-out clause which was duly exercised, but Alex Hawkridge contends to this day that Ayrton handled the whole situation with a lack of delicacy. Although Peter Warr might have thought this was non-

Segafredo
Candy
MAGIRUS
Candy
19
SERGIO TACCHINI

Hotel Mirabeau
Marlboro
MAGNETI MARELLI
Segafredo

olivetti
LONGINES

Left: *Lost in thought. Analysing the Olivetti/Longines timing screen by the pit wall at Detroit, 1984.*

Early laps at Detroit, '84. Senna's Toleman leads Martin Brundle's Tyrrell, Thierry Boutsen's Arrows, the Ferrari of René Arnoux, Stefan Bellof's Tyrrell and Ayrton's Toleman team-mate, Johnny Cecotto.

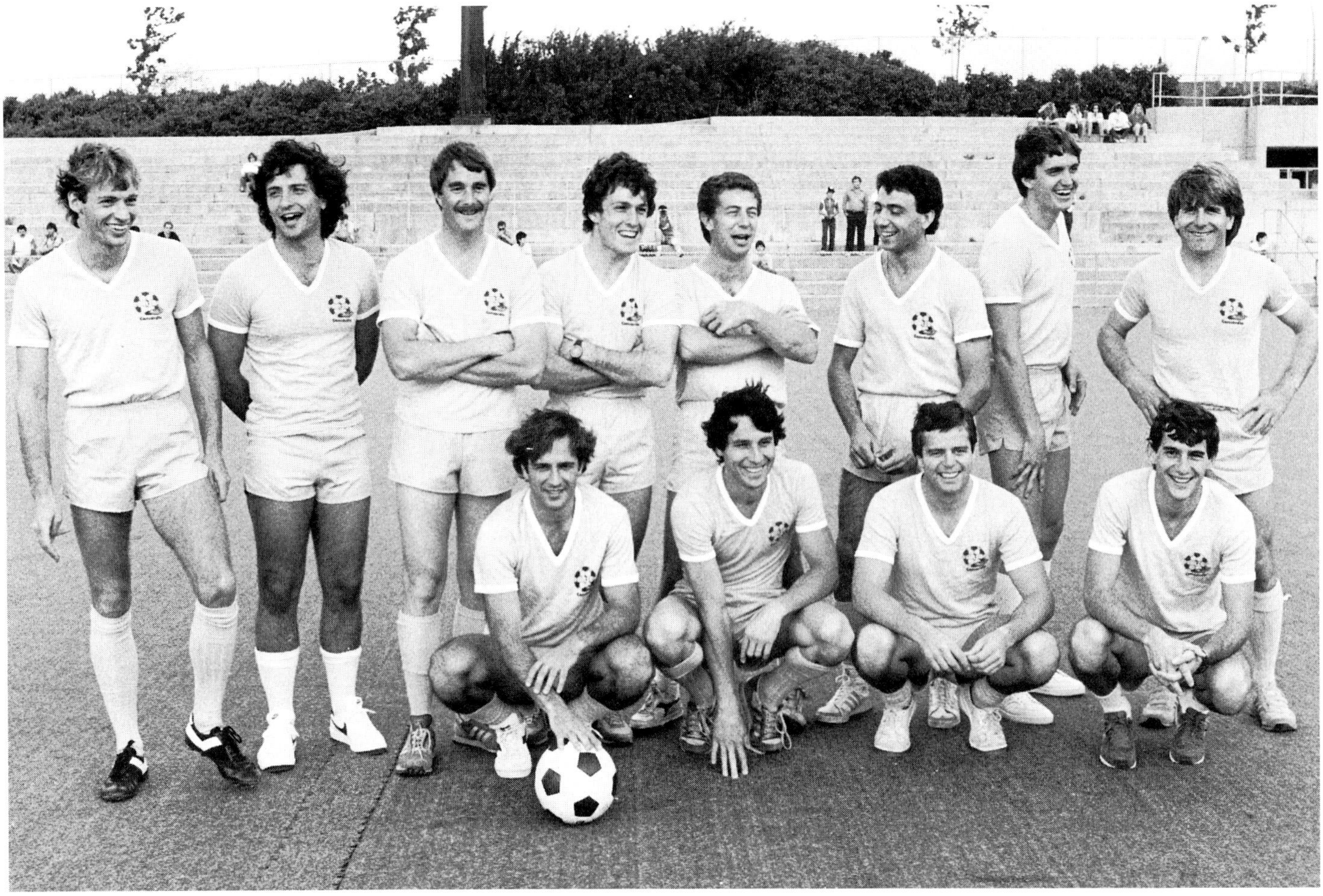

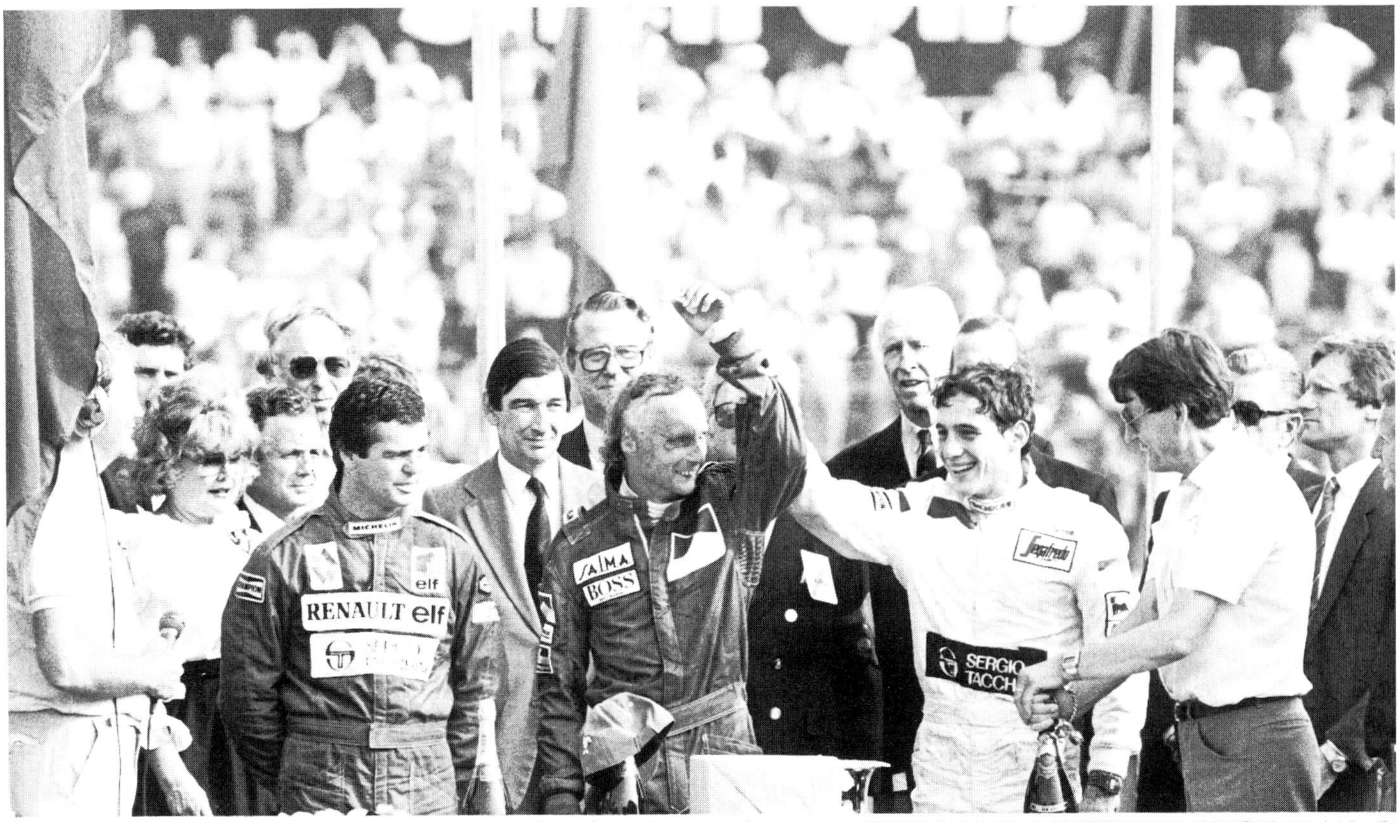
MICHELIN
RENAULT elf
BOSS
SERGIO
TACCH

Left: *Pre-Canadian Grand Prix football match, 1984: Ayrton* (front row, extreme right) *is alongside Derek Warwick.*

Below left: *Victory rostrum at the 1984 British Grand Prix. Senna* (right) *has just brought his Toleman home third behind Niki Lauda's winning McLaren and the Renault of Derek Warwick* (left).

sense at the time, those who saw the Lotus team-manager's face in 1987, when it became clear that Ayrton was not staying on for a fourth year, would have concluded that 'what goes around, comes around'. Yet Senna remains enigmatic on the subject and one is left with the strong impression that he wants to brush the precise details of his departure from Toleman under the carpet. To him it's just history, a detail from the past, buried in the deeper recesses of his mind.

Hawkridge really got the Brazilian's attention when he suspended him from the Italian Grand Prix at Monza – Stefan Johansson stood in for him and finished fourth – but he was back behind the wheel of the TG184 for the European Grand Prix at the new Nürburgring. He became embroiled in a multiple shunt at the first corner there, but rounded off the year in glorious style when his Toleman-Hart swept home imperi-

Opposite: *Exit, stage right: Ayrton's Toleman vaults into retirement over the right-front wheel of Keke Rosberg's Williams-Honda on the opening corner of the 1984 Grand Prix of Europe at the new Nürburgring.*

Below right: *Familiar company. Lauda clinches the World Championship, Estoril, '84. John Barnard* (far left), *Prost and Ron Dennis share the celebrations. Ayrton* (right) *was third behind the McLarens on his last outing for Toleman.*

ously at Estoril, third only to the McLaren-TAGs of Prost and new World Champion Lauda.

Even in 1988, when I suggested to him that, legal wrangling aside, he had left Toleman because their technical capabilities fell short of his own personal aspirations, he rejected the contention – albeit enigmatically. 'That's not correct,' he replied. 'I don't know whether it's worth going back that much, I'm not really interested. Just say that I actually left Toleman not because of technical things, but because of other reasons. I was actually very happy to stay and carry on my career with the people there. I thought they were competent and good to give me the opportunity to learn. So that was not the reason.'

In the next breath he explained his move to Lotus as 'the right direction' at the time, so one is bound to consider other factors when attempting to analyse why he exercised his release option. Looking back, when Toleman split with Pirelli and changed to Michelin, the Italian tyre company's door slammed very firmly behind them. Then, at the end of 1984, Michelin withdrew and Goodyear, overburdened with existing commitments, in addition to taking on former prestige Michelin runners like McLaren and Renault, just didn't have the capacity to supply Toleman as well. Hawkridge was advised in good time by Akron that this would be the case, so perhaps Senna read the way the situation was developing well in advance and opted for a move. In any case, the Lotus-Renault package had looked consistently promising in the hands of Elio de Angelis and Nigel Mansell over the previous couple of seasons – and, up to that point, neither of those drivers was perceived to be in the same class as Senna.

Peter Warr told author Doug Nye in his book *Theme Lotus:* 'Colin Chapman used to say that in any one year there are three, possibly four drivers in the running for the World Championship who always had to be regarded as natural Grand Prix winners. Our drivers, when I returned to Lotus in 1982, didn't figure in that elite group. In effect, we had two number twos and it stayed that way until 1985 when we took on Ayrton Senna. His class was so obvious that, when he joined us that

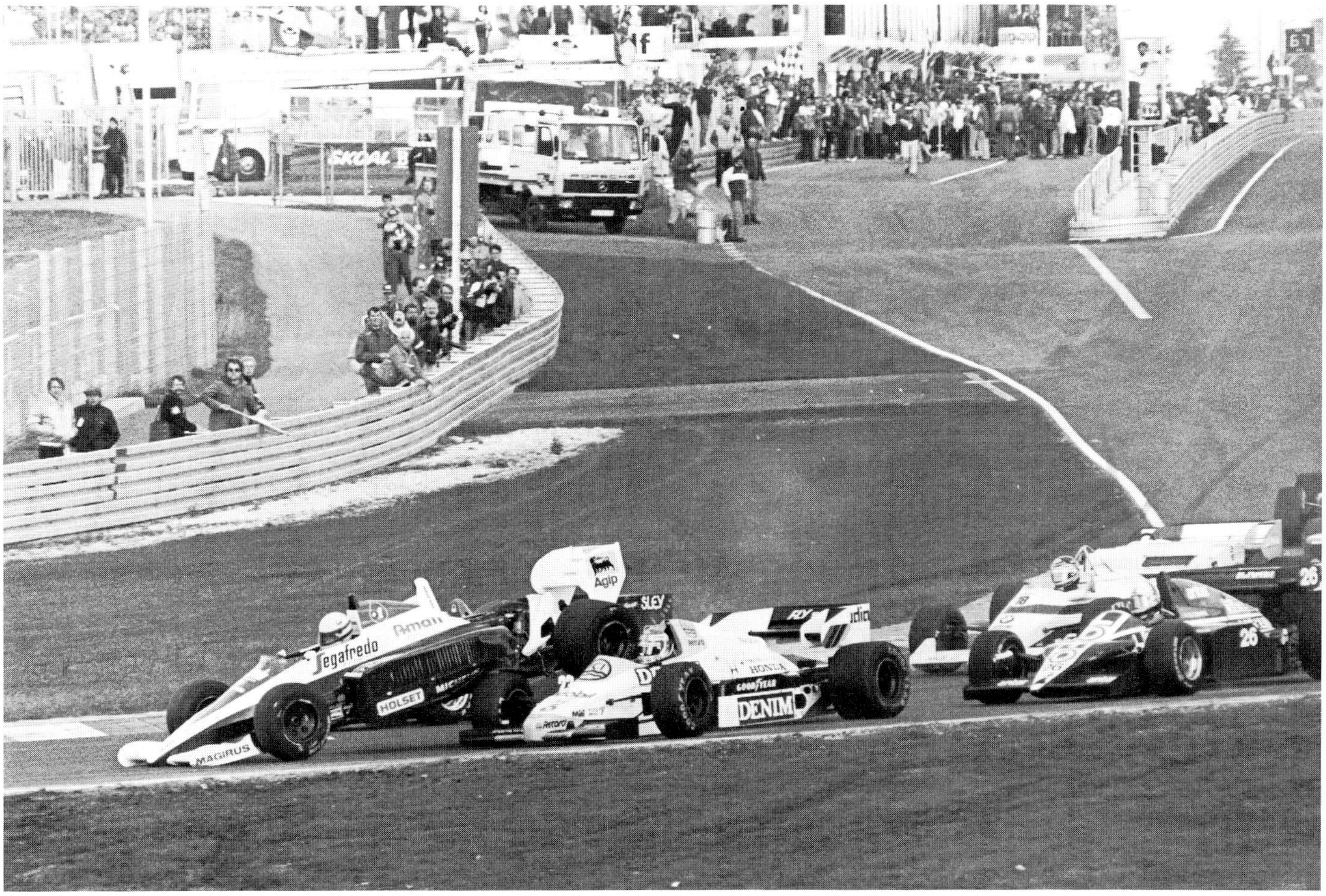
Segafredo
Agip
HOLSET
MAGIRUS
DENIM
GOODYEAR

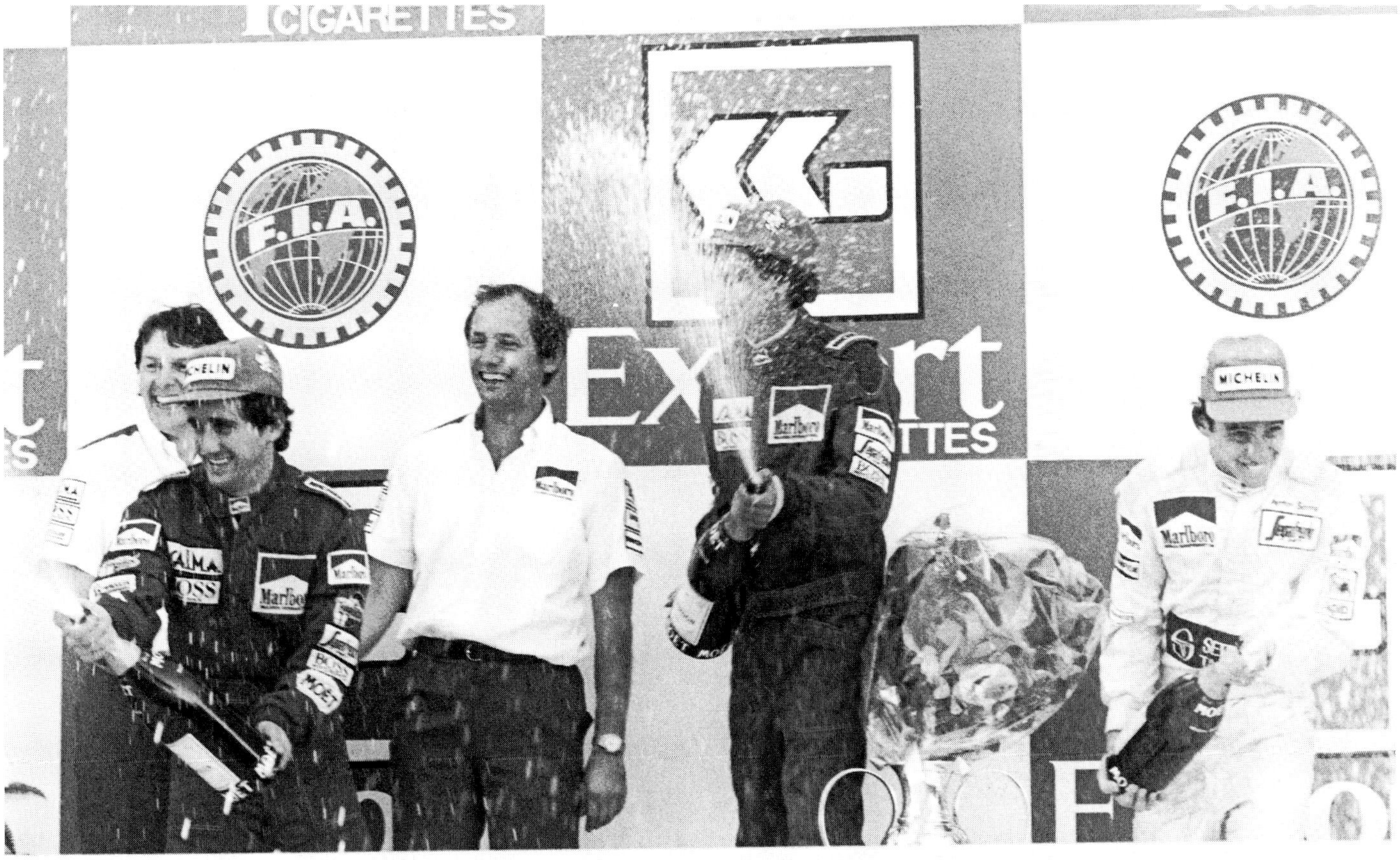
CIGARETTES
F.I.A.
F.I.A.
MICHELIN
Marlboro

Opposite: *Roadside advertising hoardings in Rio kept Ayrton and his sponsors in the forefront of attention!*

Below right: *Lotus debut. Leading Elio de Angelis round the Autodromo Riocentro during the 1985 Brazilian Grand Prix. Ayrton retired, leaving his Italian colleague to finish third.*

season, I had offered him number one status, with Elio to decide if he wanted to stay, but Ayrton turned it down, preferring to be joint number one in what was still only his second season of F1 racing, so that he could learn the trade ... but he soon made it clear that he was the number one out on the track.'

It was typical of Senna's analytical off-circuit approach that he wanted to handle his first season in a front-line team as shrewdly as possible, turning the situation to his best advantage. He was quicker than de Angelis from the outset, yet ironically Elio opened the year with a third place at Rio, where Ayrton retired. Then came Estoril – in the pouring rain. Senna, the newcomer, scarcely put a wheel out of line to win brilliantly in streaming wet conditions. He was on the verge of unlocking that enormous potential.

His first season at Lotus was not without its problems, however. Alain Prost criticised him roundly for what the Frenchman regarded as his blocking tactics at Imola, where the two of them battled long and hard for the lead of the San Marino Grand Prix. Prost was eventually first past the flag, after Senna ran out of fuel, but the McLaren-TAG was subsequently found to be slightly underweight at post-race scrutineering. It was disqualified, handing victory to none other than de Angelis in the other Lotus. Later Senna would also lead the British Grand Prix commandingly, only for his 97T to run out of fuel again, allowing Prost through to an unchallenged win. These performances gave rise to speculation that Ayrton had simply been winding up the boost pressure in a desperate bid to lead the two races. On closer examination, that contention short-changed the Brazilian's common sense. At Imola his Lotus had been fitted with the less fuel-efficient Renault EF4 engine rather than the newer EF15 (which was installed in his team-mate's car), while at Silverstone a broken sensor in the electronic management system caused one bank of cylinders to lurch onto full-rich, destroying his carefully planned

John Player Special
JPS. Sabor e emoção
Acelere, Ayrton.

John Player Special

First Grand Prix win. Ayrton masters Estoril in the Lotus 97T to win the 1985 Portuguese Grand Prix.

consumption calculations.

Senna recalls Silverstone as one of his most satisfying races, even though it didn't produce a firm result. 'If you have a good car, then you enjoy yourself,' he later reflected. 'At Silverstone in 1985 my Lotus was running really well. OK, it failed to finish, but I came away satisfied because I had been running strong and fast, in complete control of what I was doing.' He contrasted that outing with his third-place finish at Monaco the following year, behind the McLaren-TAGs of Prost and Keke Rosberg: 'Sure, I was on the podium in third place, behind the two McLarens, but the car was a disaster to drive and it was a tremendously hard race. I did not feel particularly happy about it.'

There were other disappointments in 1985, notably suffering an engine failure at Monaco after qualifying superbly on pole. He had momentarily over-revved the engine, during the race morning warm-up; the team, already working flat-out to change the Renault V6 in Elio's 97T, asked him if he would race it anyway. He did so, but he was sufficiently shrewd to realise that he had done damage to the engine that was potentially terminal – and so it proved.

None the less, Senna's second Grand Prix win was to come at Spa that year, where he headed Nigel Mansell's Williams FW10 home. He then took second billing to the Englishman in the Grand Prix of Europe at Brands Hatch and failed to finish at both Kyalami and Adelaide. The latter race, in fact, produced an untypically erratic performance by Lotus's new star, which not only encompassed a couple of wild excursions off the circuit, but also saw him wiping off the fins of his nose against the back of Rosberg's winning Williams. Eventually the 97T's Renault engine spewed most of a piston into its inlet tract and Ayrton's most inconsistent F1 race was over. To this day, nobody has ever been quite sure why Senna was so wild and unrestrained on that particular day, although it has been suggested that a slight ear infection, resulting from a water-

Player Special
John Player
Special
OLYMPUS
12
elf
RENAULT

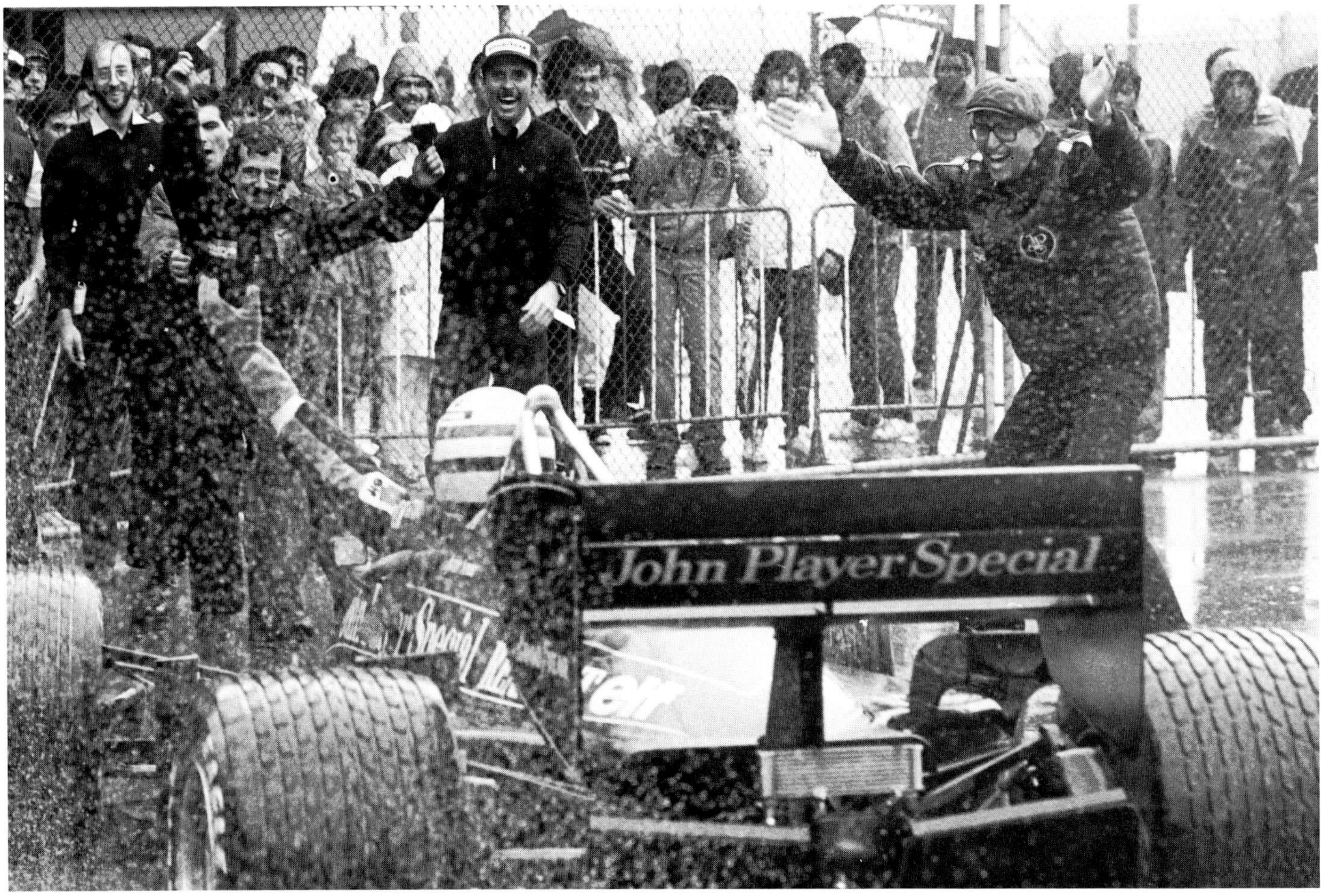
John Player Special

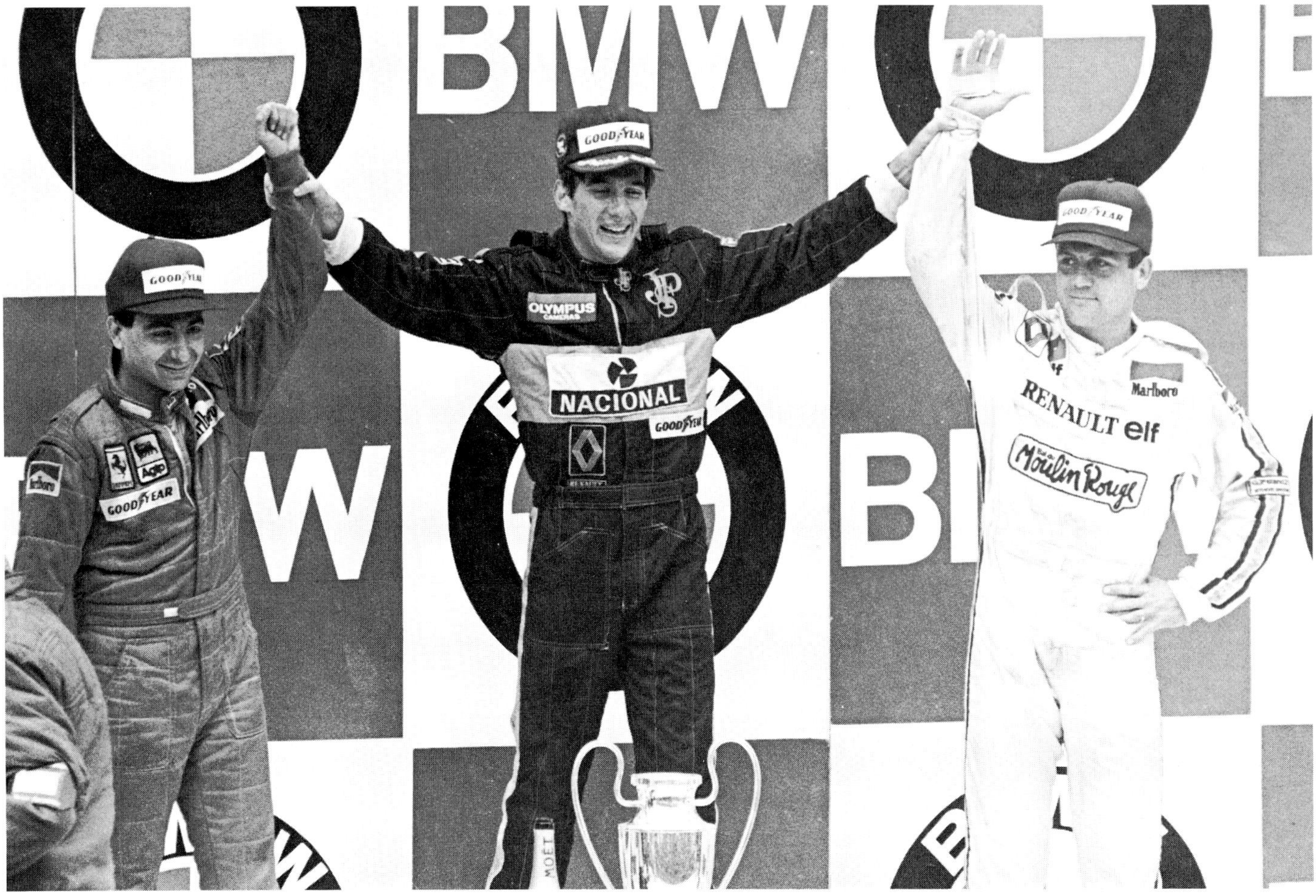
BMW
GOOD YEAR
OLYMPUS
NACIONAL
RENAULT elf
Moulin Rouge
Marlboro

Opposite: *A jubilant Ayrton swings into the scrutineering bay at Estoril to be greeted by Peter Warr* (right) *and tyre fitters Clive Hicks and Kenny Szymanski.*

Below left: *On the rostrum at Estoril with Michele Alboreto (second) and Patrick Tambay (third).*

skiing accident while he was on holiday in Mauritius, might have upset his finely honed sense of balance. Ayrton ended up fourth in the 1985 World Championship, on 38 points; Prost won the title with 73 points.

Senna's first season at Lotus had been moderately successful, but nowhere near as productive as he would have liked. It had, however, helped him to reach two conclusions. First, he now wanted to take over the mantle of undisputed number one driver for 1986. Second, since Team Lotus was demonstrably incapable of producing two reliably competitive cars to the same technical standard, he did not want a number two who was going to deflect the team's resources from his own efforts. This single-mindedness was to lead to a major controversy over the question of Derek Warwick's inclusion in the team.

The Englishman was facing F1 unemployment, now that Renault was withdrawing its factory team from F1, and Peter Warr was anxious to include him in the Lotus line-up. Warr remained convinced that Warwick would dutifully play second fiddle to Senna, but Ayrton was not so sure, contract or no contract. Inwardly, he felt that Derek would not really be happy fulfilling a supporting role, and foregoing access to the spare car, after having a sniff of success with Renault.

Warr spent a long time trying to argue Senna out of his position, to the accompaniment of critical voices from the British press (including the author's) who felt that the Lotus team-manager was allowing his authority to be undermined by his number one driver. Senna, having already had a rough ride from the English media over the manner of his departure from Toleman, wasn't at all amused by the fuss. Indeed, there is still evidence that the rift between him and the fourth estate has never fully healed.

Eventually, Lotus settled on a compromise candidate, F3 graduate Johnny Dumfries. The aristocratic Scot was destined to do an unobtrusive and workmanlike job in the second car,

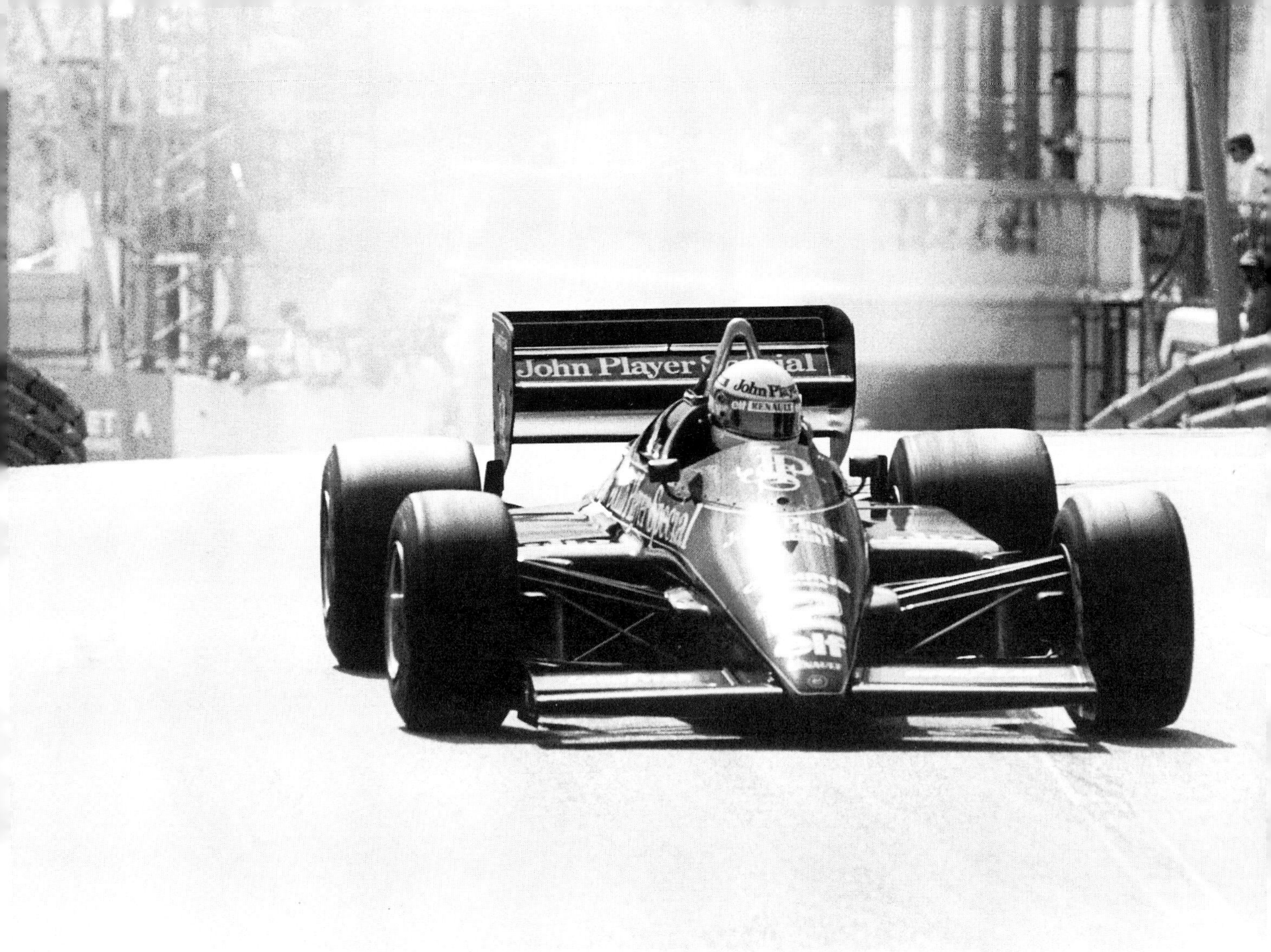

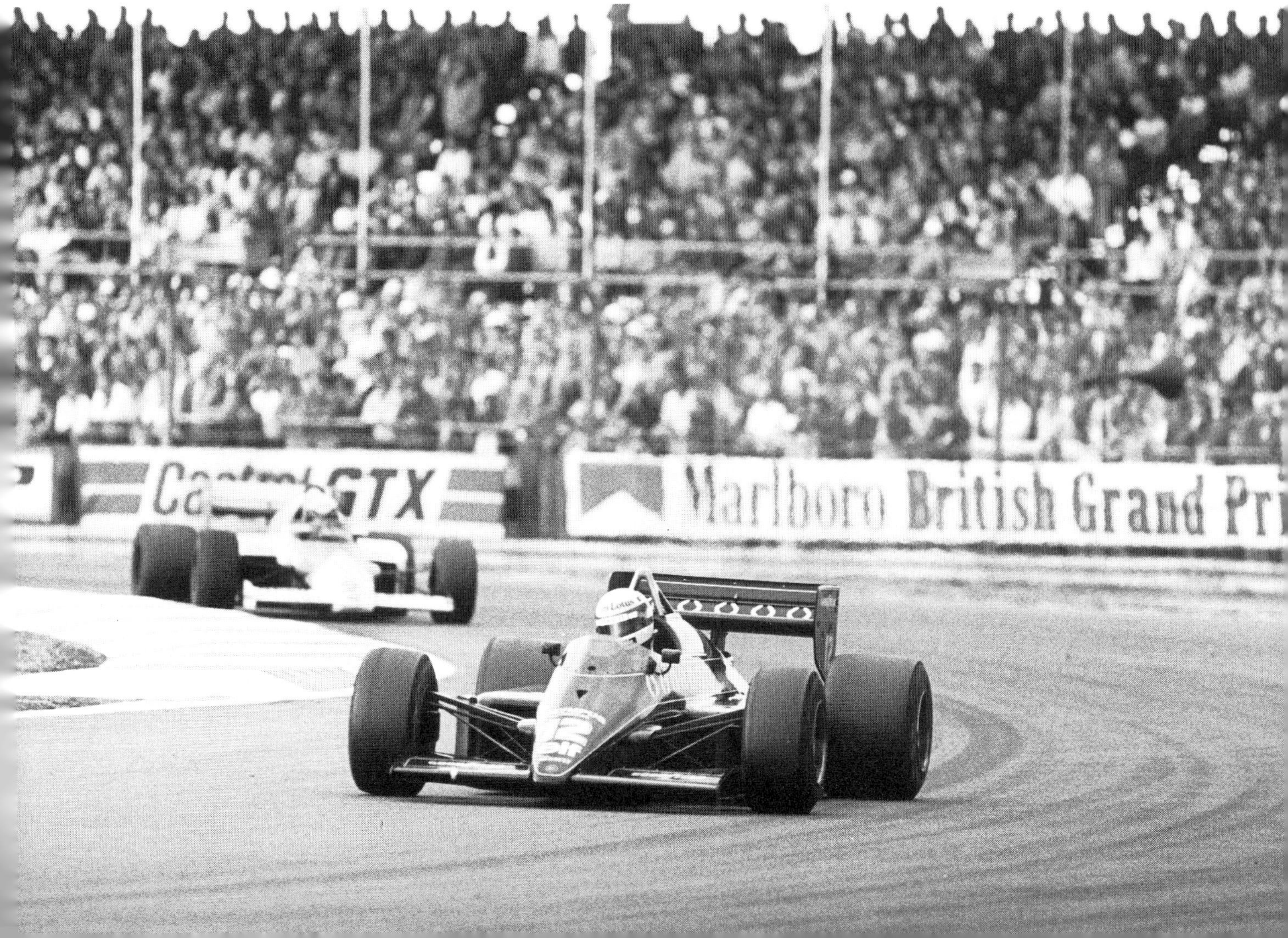

GTX
Marlboro British Grand

Left: *Blown engine, Monaco, 1985. Ayrton knew he was vulnerable, having over-revved the Renault V6 turbo during the race morning warm-up.*

Below left: *Ayrton leads Alain, British Grand Prix, 1985. Senna believes this to have been one of his very best races, but his efforts were thwarted when the Renault engine's electronic management system went haywire and he ran out of fuel, allowing Prost's McLaren unchallenged victory.*

Above: *The Belgian Grand Prix, scene of his second win of 1985: sweeping through Eau Rouge, his Lotus's skid plates kicking up a shower of sparks.*

never giving Ayrton a moment's worry. On reflection, one can state unequivocally that Ayrton had absolutely nothing at all against Warwick personally; his concern was basically about Lotus's engineering shortcomings.

For 1986 Gérard Ducarouge penned the new Lotus 98T which, powered by the latest, greatly modified version of the Renault EF15 V6, was now equipped with a highly promising pneumatic valve-closing system. This allowed the engine speed to be increased from 11,000 to 12,500 rpm. Thus armed, Senna qualified nine times in pole position, yet he added only two more Grand Prix victories to his tally. One success was through the streets of Detroit, where his delicate touch and precise throttle control reaped benefits; the other was a split-second win over Nigel Mansell's Williams-Honda at Jerez in the Spanish Grand Prix. It didn't take a clairvoyant to see that a Honda engine was needed if a driver was to run consistently at the front of the Grand Prix field.

By now Senna was sharing a large house in the Esher stockbroker belt with his old pal Mauricio Gugelmin and his wife Stella. It was a comfortably relaxed and familiar environment for the young man, who still didn't really enjoy being away from his family and friends in Brazil. The talk was of motor racing, techniques and deals, Ayrton spending long evenings analysing page after page of the Longines individual lap-time print-outs from the various races, and only allowing himself a break from matters motor racing to fly his scale model aeroplanes, his fast-mushrooming off-track preoccupation.

'I first got involved with them through a friend in 1985, at around the time of the Brands Hatch Grand Prix,' he explains, 'and I've got more and more involved ever since. They have 10 or 20 cc engines, running on special fuel and, yes, while there are competitions in which you can take part, I just fly them for pure pleasure.' Those who have seen him putting his planes through their paces will testify to a level of daring and

Below right: *Beaming with delight at an early Formula Ford victory, 1981.*

Below left: *At the wheel of the FF2000 Van Diemen, Mallory Park, 1982.*

Ayrton's West Surrey Engineering Ralt leads Martin Brundle's similar Eddie Jordan-entered machine at Silverstone (bottom) *during their season-long tussle for the 1983 Marlboro British F3 crown.*

MONROE
Marlboro
Segafredo
ZANETTI

Agip
19
Segafredo
ERREGI

First F1 race, with the Toleman TG183B at Rio, 1984.

Below: *Jerez 1986: Ayrton's Lotus just managed to hold off a late charge from Mansell's Williams to record Grand Prix win number three.*

Overleaf: *Ayrton's 1986 French Grand Prix ended early in the race when he flew off the road on another driver's dropped oil.*

NACIONAL
Player
RENAULT
elf
NACIONAL

Ayrton Senna
Turbo
er Special
REN
12
DeL

He was off the road in practice in Mexico, 1987, battling to keep his slim chance of the championship open to the bitter end (left).

Below left: *Signing autographs for the fans at Monza, 1987.*

Below: *First win for McLaren. After disappointment in Brazil, Ayrton dominated the San Marino Grand Prix.*

Shell
Marlboro
Marlboro
BOSS
MEN'S FASHION

Left: *Off-track obsession: Ayrton with one of his radio-controlled model planes.*

Below: *Victory at Montreal, 1988.*

Overleaf: *Ayrton Senna and Honda Marlboro McLaren: record-breakers in 1988.*

Marlboro
POWERED by
HONDA
Senna
BOSS
Marlboro
HONDA
HONDA
NACIONAL
Marlboro
Shell

TAG
HEUER
HONDA
12

benetton
Marlboro
benetton
GOODYEAR
USF&G
27
USF&G
17

Left: *The race of his life? Senna battles through the field after a disastrous start to the Japanese Grand Prix. Having passed Patrese and Nannini, Ayrton sets his sights on Boutsen, Alboreto and Warwick.*

Below: *Old friend Thierry Boutsen christens a jubilant 1988 World Champion.*

Portrait of a champion: Ayrton obviously still full of emotion shortly after the 1988 Japanese Grand Prix.

commitment matched only by his exploits behind the wheel of a Grand Prix car ...

The 1986 season developed into a three-way battle for the championship between Nelson Piquet, Nigel Mansell and McLaren's Alain Prost, the Frenchman slipping through to grab his second successive title from the warring Williams-Honda teamsters at the very last race of the year. The Frenchman finished the season on 70 points, Senna trailing in fourth once more with 55 points. By the end of the season Ayrton Senna had reached something of a turning-point. Three years into his F1 career there was no doubt that a mere four Grand Prix victories were scarcely an accurate representation of either his ability level or his potential. But, as he would remark frequently, 'Every time I go out and race, I am there only because I believe it is possible to win.'

Mansell and Piquet had proved that, all else being equal, a Honda turbo was fast becoming a necessary prerequisite for any sustained success. Lotus therefore finalised a deal to acquire Honda engines in 1987, at least partly in exchange for agreeing to take Japanese journeyman Satoru Nakajima as Senna's team-mate. Moreover, Lotus had a trick or two up their sleeve in the form of the computer-controlled active suspension system which, it was hoped, would give the new 99T a winning edge over the Williams-Hondas. But as early as the eve of his 1987 Monaco victory, Senna had not only assessed the car's potential *vis-à-vis* the Williams FW11Bs, but was also almost certainly on the verge of concluding a deal to move to McLaren in 1988.

With the benefit of hindsight, the remarks made by Senna in an interview I taped with him at Monaco are even more illuminating and significant than they seemed at the time. In response to my asking him whether he considered this year (1987) as a development season for the active suspension, on which he could build to win the title in 1988, he responded with a firm 'no'. I then asked him whether he felt he could win

Above: *Closest win. Holding off Mansell's Williams-Honda to take the 1986 Spanish Grand Prix at Jerez by one-hundredth of a second.*

It's all a bit of a strain!

1986: maturing fast now. No longer the wide-eyed young kid of three years before ...

Above left: *Off-duty, fascinated by a radio-controlled model car.*

Fourth career win: chequered flag at Detroit, *1986.* Below: *leading René Arnoux's Ligier in the early stages, before Senna's Lotus suffered a tyre deflation.*

Right: *Inherited victory. Ayrton at Monaco, 1987, with the active suspension Lotus-Honda 99T.*

Below right: *Victory rostrum celebration in the Principality – showering the champagne with Alboreto, while Piquet tries to hide.*

the 1987 title. A longer pause – followed by another 'no'.

It quickly became clear to Senna that, from an aerodynamic standpoint, the Lotus-Honda wasn't up to the standard of the Williams, while the sheer volume of technical input from the active suspension system simply could not be monitored and analysed quickly enough during the crowded racing calendar. He was to win at Monaco, but only after Mansell's Williams retired, and while the benefits of the active suspension system made life less stressful over the corrugations of Detroit, where he scored his only other victory of the year, in general terms the Lotus could not offer that elusive, winning edge.

Ayrton and the team were undeniably happy that the system had at least been reliable from the outset, but there were clearly other aspects of the 99T's performance that lagged behind the front-line opposition. 'At the start of the active suspension programme we were perhaps a little over-optimistic about the length of time it would take to produce a measurable performance advantage,' Senna explained. 'The season was an enormous challenge for everybody at Lotus, with a new car, new engine, new suspension and new gearbox, so we anticipated many problems. But we decided to race the active system at Rio and, while it was reliable, I felt the car was moving around too much.

'We improved it considerably in time for Imola, and although we faced a major handling imbalance at Spa, by the time we got to qualifying at Monaco I felt it was working very well. The system has enormous potential and each time I drove the car I realised how little I really understood about the car's set-up. You see, it provides so much information that you could relate to what you recall in a particular corner, for example, and it provides you with a lot of material that you would not have otherwise appreciated.

'However, the system is so complex that there is always scope for improvement, even when it is working well. If we were using the conventional passive suspension, then I think

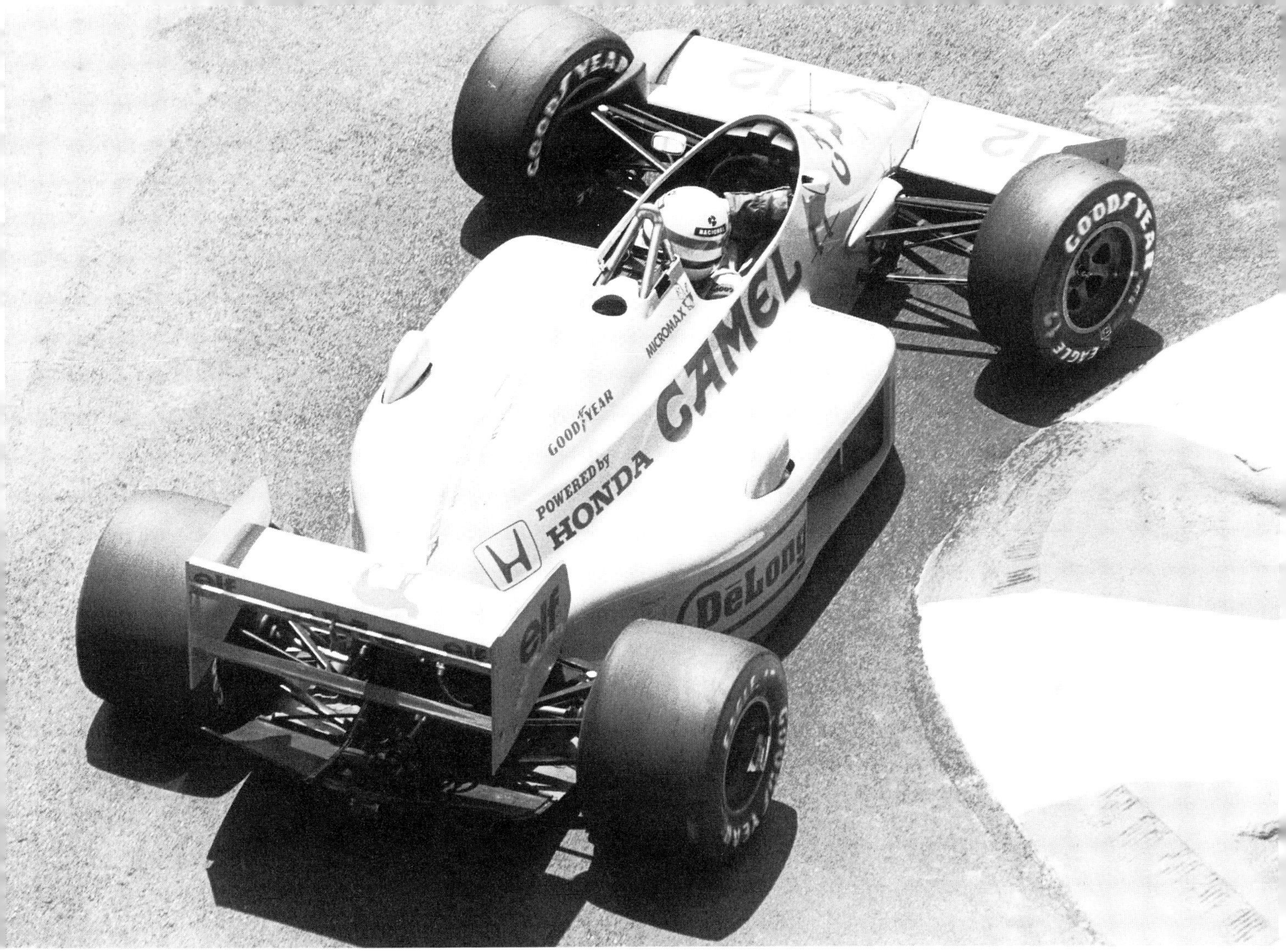
CAMEL
POWERED by
HONDA
GOODYEAR
MICROMAX
elf
12

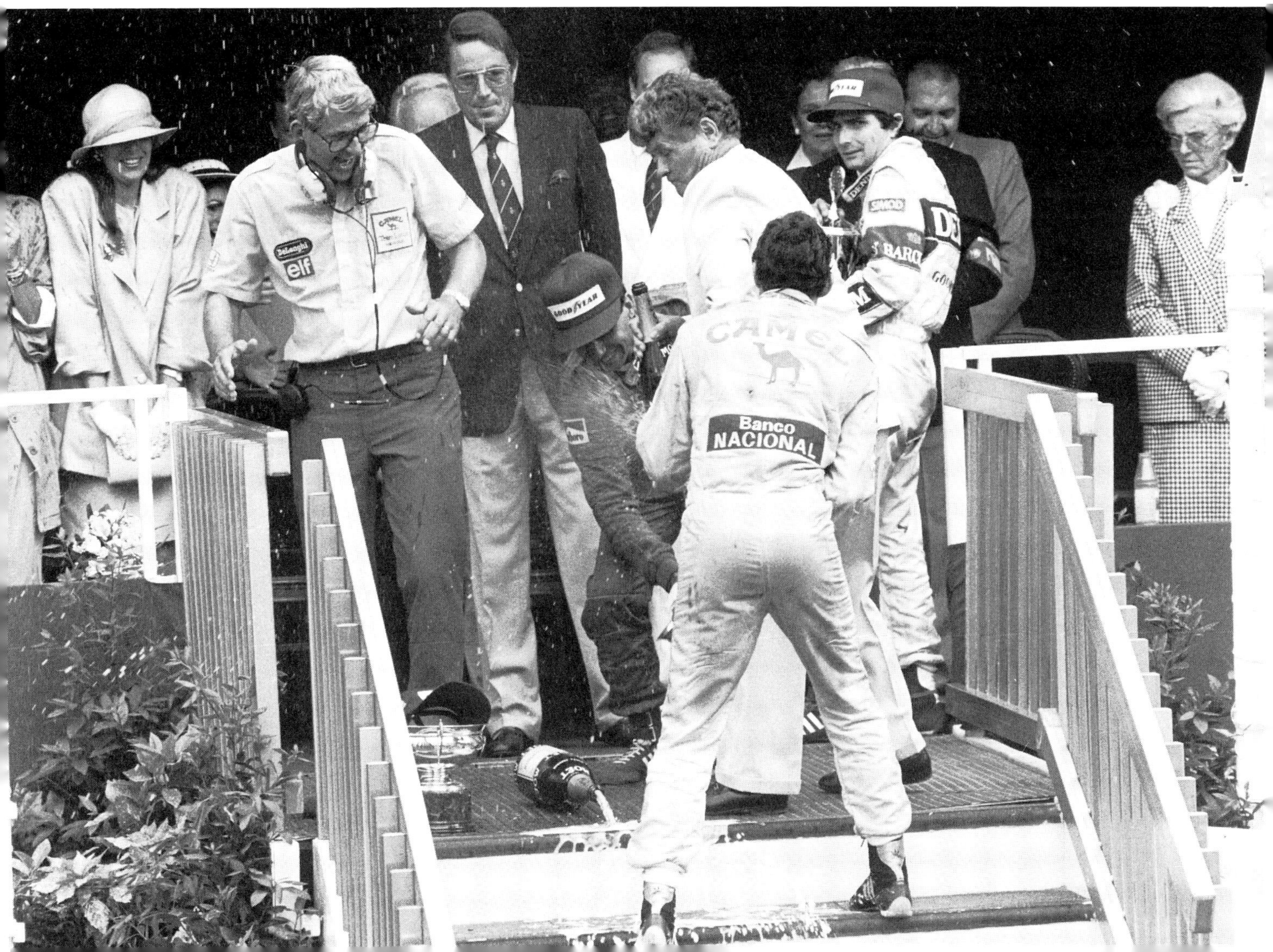
CAMEL
Banco
NACIONAL
GOODYEAR
elf

we might have discovered that our other problems with the car would actually have been greater.'

This promise notwithstanding, Senna had decided on a change of team before Hockenheim and, in the week following the German race, his lawyers wrote to Team Lotus informing them of Ayrton's intention to move on for 1988. It wasn't until Monza that the F1 fraternity received official word that he would be driving a Marlboro McLaren-Honda alongside Alain Prost in 1988.

From time to time, throughout his career, even Ayrton's most ardent fans would have to concede there could occasionally be a hint of desperation about his driving, usually when things were not going his way. In 1987, as he wrestled to keep his championship hopes alive with the recalcitrant Lotus-Honda, that desperation surfaced several times.

At Hockenheim Senna attracted the wrath of Michele Alboreto – he had nearly put the Ferrari driver off the circuit by weaving on the straight – and the Italian was almost grey with indignation. (It had been the same back in '85, when Ayrton, having taken pole at Monaco, cruised round slowly on the racing line, apparently intent on spoiling the chances of his rivals Alboreto and Niki Lauda. This was one of the very few occasions in his career that I actually saw Lauda lose his temper.) 'With his talent, he just doesn't have to do that,' Alboreto complained, although it has to be said that Michele is hardly an innocent when it comes to adopting awkward racing lines. But Senna did just that at Hockenheim, surviving to finish second despite his Lotus 'collapsing' onto its 'reserve' springs after the active suspension sprang a leak and lost all its hydraulic fluid. It was a real never-say-die, dogged performance by the Brazilian: he just didn't know how to give up.

Alboreto settled the score at the Osterreichring, brake-testing Senna to send him scuttling for a replacement nose cone, but at Monza his heroic gamble of a non-stop run almost paid off. With seven laps to run he was hanging on just ahead of

Unlocking the key to '88. Ayrton in company with Alain Prost, Ron Dennis and Honda's Yoshitoshi Sakurai at the McLaren-Honda announcement, Monza, 1987.

Piquet's Williams when he slid onto the dirt at the Parabolica, allowing the other Brazilian through to victory. Ayrton recovered to finish second, only 1.8s down. He tried for a non-stop run at Jerez, as well, holding up a great queue of slower cars, before fading to fifth. It was a performance which seemed a bit extreme, to say the least, even attracting admonishing remarks from former World Champion Jackie Stewart.

Probably the most memorable episode of that action-packed 1987 season came at Spa, where Nigel Mansell took him off on

Marlboro
HONDA

Grand alliance. Prost and Senna with the MP4/4-Honda at Rio, prior to the Brazilian Grand Prix.

the opening lap and, the Englishman having decided that the incident was Senna's fault, later attempted to thump him when they squared up to each other in the Team Lotus pit garage. Ayrton also shunted hard during practice at Mexico City, where his title chances finally evaporated, and he rounded off his Lotus career by being disqualified from second place in Adelaide, where the 99T's extra front brake cooling ducts were deemed to infringe the permissible coachwork dimensions.

For 1988, he faced the prospect of battling with Alain Prost, a rival he admitted he respected 'not only for his driving, but for his whole manner, his achievement, his behaviour'. He was also striding into Prost's personal enclave, where the Frenchman was popularly established. Many people felt that Ayrton would have the upper hand from race to race, but that the canny Prost would have the overall edge, taken throughout the championship campaign.

Sure enough, Prost kicked off with a win at Rio, the new MP4/4-Honda turbo demonstrating a level of technical superiority such as to make the World Championship contest the McLaren team's personal property. Psychology played a major part in the relationship between these two outstandingly talented drivers who, while sharing the same competitive urges, are as different as chalk from cheese. On the one hand, Prost: gregarious, easy-going, imbued with a wicked sense of humour and with a relaxed manner thinly concealing his professionalism and commitment. On the other, Senna: obsessive, intense, almost dour, and totally absorbed in the technocratic challenge of making a Grand Prix car operate to its absolute optimum.

Ayrton qualified on pole at Rio, but gearchange problems spiked his challenge even before the start. He was eventually black-flagged and disqualified for changing to the spare car after the green flag had been waved to indicate the start of the pre-race parade lap. So Prost finished the day nine points ahead.

At Imola Ayrton was on pole again and now showed what he

Marlboro
Marlboro
Marlboro
HONDA
11
Shell
Shell

Left: *Prost leads Senna in the early stages at Montreal. Once Ayrton was through, he didn't wait around for his team-mate.*

With Osamu Goto, Honda's F1 project leader, on the pit wall at the Hungaroring, 1988.

Marlboro
Marlboro
valentino
valentino
Marlboro
12
Marlboro
Shell
GOODYEAR
EAGLE
USF&G
USF&G
17

Out ahead, alone in the lead at Monaco ...

... until he hit that wall. Derek Warwick, passing, must have suppressed a smile.

could do. He led from start to finish, contending with a slight gear-linkage gremlin which almost pitched him into a spin at one point. But Prost came back to win at Monaco after Ayrton, the race apparently in the bag, slid into the wall at the Portier right-hander, removing his McLaren's left-front wheel.

'I'd driven almost the perfect race,' he reflects, 'probably the best I'd ever done in terms of qualifying, race performance and car set-up – until the end. There were some reasons behind it, of which I was aware, but to which I wasn't reacting. Earlier, I had a moment in Casino Square when the car jumped out of gear as I began to relax. I nearly hit the barrier. I got myself back into a rhythm, but then the same process happened again and this time it caught me out.'

Later, after clinching the World Championship at Suzuka, Ayrton conceded that Monaco was the turning-point of the year. He considered that, psychologically, he changed a lot after that mistake woke him up: 'I have to say it also brought me closer to God than I had ever been, and has changed my life completely ...'

In terms of accepted professionalism, however, his decision to return immediately to his nearby flat – his European base when away fron his beloved Brazil – amounted to a major breach of team etiquette. For over three hours Ron Dennis had no first-hand information as to what had caused the shunt. The team was not amused, although Senna later professed not to know what on earth all the fuss was about. His supporters would argue that this intensely egocentric streak helps make him the driver he unquestionably is. The fact remains, though, that the team was extremely disappointed with his behaviour on that particular occasion.

They were not often disappointed, of course. Prost, meanwhile, inherited victory at Monaco and went on to beat Ayrton in Mexico, the Brazilian hampered by a faulty pop-off valve and higher-than-expected fuel consumption. Four races down, and Prost had won three of them.

Alain was relieved, but knew pretty well what to expect in

Below: *Grappling with gearchange gremlins, Ayrton had to follow his team-mate home in the 1988 French Grand Prix at Paul Ricard.*

Right: *With his brother, Leonardo.*

Shaving the walls (below right) *in downtown Motown, heading for his Detroit Grand Prix hat-trick.*

Montreal and Detroit, where Senna's audacity in traffic was certain to pay dividends. The Frenchman led initially in Canada, only to be muscled aside and then dropped as Ayrton shimmered through gaps that hardly looked as though they were there. Alain had been around for too long to be interested in heroics of that sort. He was second in both races.

Gearchange problems intervened again at Paul Ricard, where Ayrton was not only beaten to pole position by Prost, but headed across the line at the end of a race which had seen the Frenchman snatch the lead in a brilliantly opportunist manoeuvre, as the two McLarens threaded their path through the back-markers.

olivetti
LONGINES
GOOD YEAR
Shell
BOSS
MEN'S FASHION
Marlboro
McLAREN INTERNATIONAL
HONDA

PEN TO PUBLIC RESTROOMS & REFRESHMENTS HOTDOGS DRINKS
EniChem
Marlboro
HONDA
12
Shell

Senna had been trailing Prost in the championship points table ever since Rio, but the next couple of races would see his title aspirations rise dramatically. Moreover, there was to be a certain irony in the way the pattern of the season developed for Prost. Never one to conceal his dislike of racing in the rain, the Frenchman was dealt a most unfortunate hand at both Silverstone and Hockenheim when the British and German Grands Prix became the first wet races for three years – since Ayrton Senna won at Estoril for Lotus, in fact!

At Silverstone, major aerodynamic revisions to the turbo ducting within the MP4/4 side pods somewhat scrambled the team's technical progress throughout qualifying, leaving Senna and Prost on the second row of the grid behind the Ferraris of Gerhard Berger and Michele Alboreto. During qualifying Ayrton's remarkable qualities of icy cool were put on public display when he twice pirouetted the McLaren-Honda exiting Stowe corner. Before the tyre smoke had cleared, he engaged a lower gear and accelerated away from the incident, the McLaren having never come to a standstill ...

The race itself was controversial for the McLaren team, although not on Ayrton's part. In streaming rain, he tailed Berger's Ferrari for the first 14 laps before ducking through into the lead, under braking for the Woodcote chicane. The depth of Prost's problems that day can be realised from the fact that Ayrton lapped him as he slipped ahead of Berger. In fact, if it hadn't been for Alain giving him room as he came through under braking, the two MP4/4s might well have collided. Prost simply could not get his car to work in the appalling conditions and he eventually chose to retire after a humiliating midfield performance. Clearly, there was something very badly wrong with his chassis set-up, but he made no apology for his decision to withdraw. Typical Prost, he remained very much his own man.

It was much the same story at Hockenheim. Ayrton ran away into the distance, but this time Alain salvaged his reputa-

Ayrton excelled in the patchy wet conditions at Hockenheim to win the 1988 German Grand Prix in typically assured style.

Canon
Marlboro
Marlboro
HONDA
BARCLAY

LEYTON march HOUSE
Marlboro
Marlboro
HONDA
12
Shell
Shell

Equalling Alain! A split-second victory over his McLaren team-mate at the Hungaroring brought Senna level on points with the Frenchman. Left: *he just hangs on ahead of Mansell's Williams-Judd in the early stages.*

Below left: *Less happy. Under pressure from Ivan Capelli's March during Ayrton's troubled 1988 Portuguese Grand Prix at Estoril.*

tion with a strong second, albeit punctuated by a spin over the rain-slicked kerb at the Ostkurve. The Grand Prix action then moved behind the Iron Curtain, to the Hungaroring, where Ayrton battled furiously for pole position with the naturally aspirated Williams FW12 of Nigel Mansell and Thierry Boutsen's Benetton B188. This was one of the few circuits where the non-turbos reckoned they might have a realistic crack at the 2.5-bar/150-litre turbos, but while Mansell tailed Ayrton doggedly in the opening stages, the Englishman was suffering badly from the after-effects of a secondary chicken-pox infection and proved incapable of lasting the distance.

Prost, meanwhile, had qualified a lowly seventh. He spent the early stages of the race conserving as much fuel as he possibly could in the queue behind Senna. Alain rightly figured that his car was quicker than Ayrton's on this particular afternoon, but while keeping pace with the Brazilian might have been one thing, passing him was very definitely a different proposition. He pressed home his attack, though, and eventually managed to ease inside Ayrton, going into the downhill right-hander after the pits, as Senna was busy overtaking Philippe Alliot's Lola and Gabriele Tarquini's Coloni, who were having their own private joust.

Alain came in too quickly, on too tight a line. 'I knew he was quicker than me, so I had to get past him again at the earliest opportunity,' Ayrton explained. Prost immediately handed him back the initiative by sliding wide, away from the apex. Senna ducked round the back of his team-mate and regained the lead before the end of the corner. Prost eased back now, worried by a slight front-wheel vibration which was, in fact, nothing more than debris picked up by his tyres. In the closing moments of the race he spurted back onto Senna's tail, but there was just no way through: the two McLarens sailed past the chequered flag less than a second apart.

This was a crucial moment for Senna, the day on which he finally drew level with Prost on points. From here he went on

to win the Belgian Grand Prix at Spa, destroying Prost's challenge in a straight fight, the Frenchman's ability to respond blunted when he gambled on reducing his MP4/4's aerodynamic downforce on the grid a few minutes before the start. 'Ayrton will now be World Champion,' conceded Prost, 'and I think he fully deserves it. He has driven extremely well this season. He will be a worthy champion.'

In retrospect, Prost's declaration seems somewhat melodramatic. A few weeks later he confessed that he'd been suffering from mid-season blues, grappling with an intermittently troublesome engine and a chassis which definitely didn't feel up to scratch. Moreover, who could have foreseen, on that sunny afternoon, as Senna mastered the high-speed sweeps of Spa-Francorchamps, that the Brazilian would be away from the winner's circle for the next two months?

Monza, of course, was the one spectacular flaw in the McLaren team's otherwise impeccable display. Ayrton took the lead from the start, with Prost chasing hard, already handicapped by a slightly misfiring engine, but at least consoling himself with the fact that he had been allocated a brand new chassis for this race. Alain was eventually to retire with a rare piston failure. By this time the McLaren team-mates had raced each other into a parlous fuel situation, leaving Senna with the prospect of scraping home by a hair's breadth from the Ferraris – assuming he took the absolute maximum out of the chassis and pussy-footed with his throttle control.

That historic moment when Jean-Louis Schlesser, in the Williams, collided with Senna at the first chicane, with fractionally less than two laps left to run, will be etched in the minds of Grand Prix fans for a generation. Even Ron Dennis allowed that it had been a demonstration of the way in which Senna's supreme confidence and push in traffic could work against him. Moreover, the strategic need to shimmer through this particular gap with a sense of total urgency was of paramount importance to the race's potential outcome. Some you win, some you lose.

Senna scored a crushing victory over Prost at Spa in the Belgian Grand Prix to further strengthen his title challenge.

Its run of eleven consecutive victories broken by that Monza misfortune, the McLaren team regrouped at Estoril for the Portuguese Grand Prix, determined to restore the status quo. This time Prost started from pole position, Ayrton finding that his MP4/4's cockpit instruments were playing up through much of qualifying. There were two starts to this race, the first aborted by a multiple shunt down among the midfield runners. In the sprint to the first corner, meanwhile, Prost eased out Senna with untypical spirit, almost pushing the Brazilian onto the grass on the left-hand side of the circuit as he took the line into the turn.

Senna was not impressed. At the second start, when Alain attempted to duplicate the manoeuvre, Ayrton held him out and chopped across into the lead. Then, as Alain hurtled up onto his tail, coming out of the last right-hander to complete the opening lap, Ayrton squeezed him towards the pit wall in what was, by any standards, an extremely hazardous piece of driving. Prost kept his nerve, though, his MP4/4 skipping precariously over the bumps as he surged by into the lead. The Frenchman was never headed all the way to the flag. Ayrton, battling with poor chassis balance and blistered tyres (which forced a pit stop after contact with Mansell's Williams), wound up sixth.

The two men resolved their differences over that first-lap incident behind closed doors, Prost telling Ayrton that, frankly, he hadn't really appreciated how much he wanted to win the championship. In fact, Alain told him, he could take it if it meant driving like that. Ayrton was briefly chastened, but steadfastly refused to answer press enquiries about the exchange. 'It's over, forgotten,' he said firmly. Ron Dennis tried to appear relaxed about the episode, although he was clearly concerned. 'You've got to remember it's not a schoolgirls' tea party out there,' he told me. 'They are racing for the World Championship, for heaven's sake ...' Even so, it had been too close for comfort.

GOODYEAR
Marlboro
Shell
BOSS
Marlboro
McLAREN INTERNATIONAL

Marlboro
Shell
Shell

With the title won, Ayrton had to settle for second place behind Prost in the season's finale at Adelaide.

A week later, Prost stamped his mastery on the Spanish Grand Prix at Jerez, leading from start to finish despite the fact that Ayrton had qualified in pole position. The Brazilian wound up fourth, his fuel computer providing him with unnecessarily pessimistic information for much of the race. Speculation now centred on whether or not Prost could sustain his slender advantage in the points table, bearing in mind that, under the 'best 11 out of 16 results' rule, he was only amassing three points for each win from Spain onwards. Senna was mathematically in the stronger position.

The story ended at Suzuka, three weeks later, as recounted in the first few pages of this volume. One of the most remarkably talented yet ambiguous personalities ever to race a Grand Prix car, Ayrton Senna's genius is underpinned by an arrogant persona which craves a level of privacy impossible to achieve in such a highly conspicuous, big-money sport. Yet, for all that, few outsiders have been able to pierce the protective carapace of the Brazilian's character. As far as most of us know him, in the Grand Prix pit lane, he is the distant, coolly aloof star, always keeping part of himself back lest he reveals an area of vulnerability.

Team-mate Prost, although clearly very disappointed with the outcome of the championship, has a shrewd perception of Senna's qualities as a driver. 'What impressed me was his ability to push hard at all times and be quick in all conditions,' says the Frenchman. 'It doesn't matter whether it's a fast or slow circuit, rain, heat, traffic ... he has an enormously high degree of commitment. Our relationship has been better than perhaps I might have imagined; a bit tense to start with, but progressively improving – with one or two exceptions – through to the end of the year. But I always knew that 1988 might be difficult because he wanted the World Championship so passionately, just as I did the first time. Even now, in Adelaide, I sense that he is more relaxed now he has achieved his ambition...'

Despite his attempts to protect his personal privacy, though, Ayrton Senna makes no secret of his perfectionist approach out on the circuit. 'Of course, one always has to examine the way one's driving technique is developing, the problems you face and how to deal with them,' he says thoughtfully. 'You are changing all the time, making adjustments to your driving technique. It is a non-stop job. You keep adjusting yourself to cater for the equipment as it develops, the situations as they arise.

'When I was at Lotus or Toleman, or in F3, my only wish was to succeed, to win, so when you don't get that success, it becomes frustrating – particularly when you know you could have done better in other circumstances. But whatever I have done, I think I have always gone better and better. That's fundamental for keeping your motivation, your power to carry on. Improving, improving ... all the time.

'You never manage to achieve perfection. As hard as you try, you can never be perfect. The closer you get, the more difficult progress becomes ...'

With his first World Championship under his belt, the pressure of that quest for the Holy Grail finally released, Ayrton Senna's career stands poised to progress onward and upward. It also remains to be seen whether this complex and undeniably self-possessed man will allow himself – ever so slightly – to relax. Many believe that, if he can permit himself this luxury, Senna has the ability to release a further flood-tide of achievement and surpass his glittering F1 record to date.

AYRTON SENNA · CAREER RECORD BY JOHN TAYLOR

Kart Championship wins

1977 South American Championship
1978 South American Championship
1978 Brazilian Championship
1979 Brazilian Championship
1980 Brazilian Championship
1981 Brazilian Championship

Kart World Championship positions

1977	6th
1979	2nd
1980	2nd
1981	4th

1981

	Race	*Circuit*	*Date*	*Entrant*	*Car*	*Comment*
5	P & O Ferries FF1600, round 1	Brands Hatch	01/03/81	Van Diemen	Van Diemen RF80-Ford	*First car race*
3	Townsend-Thoresen FF1600, round 1	Thruxton	08/03/81	Van Diemen	Van Diemen RF81-Ford	
1	Townsend-Thoresen FF1600, round 2	Brands Hatch	15/03/81	Van Diemen	Van Diemen RF81-Ford	*First win*
2	Townsend-Thoresen FF1600, round 3	Mallory Park	22/03/81	Van Diemen	Van Diemen RF81-Ford	*Pole*
2	Townsend-Thoresen FF1600, round 4	Mallory Park	05/04/81	Van Diemen	Van Diemen RF81-Ford	
2	Townsend-Thoresen FF1600, round 5	Snetterton	03/05/81	Van Diemen	Van Diemen RF81-Ford	*Pole*
1	RAC FF1600, round 1	Oulton Park	24/05/81	Van Diemen	Van Diemen RF81-Ford	*Fastest lap*
1	Townsend-Thoresen FF1600, round 6	Mallory Park	25/05/81	Van Diemen	Van Diemen RF81-Ford	
1	Townsend-Thoresen FF1600, round 7	Snetterton	07/06/81	Van Diemen	Van Diemen RF81-Ford	*Fastest lap*
2	RAC FF1600, round 2	Silverstone	21/06/81	Van Diemen	Van Diemen RF81-Ford	
1	Townsend-Thoresen FF1600, round 8	Oulton Park	27/06/81	Van Diemen	Van Diemen RF81-Ford	*Fastest lap*
1	RAC FF1600, round 3	Donington Park	04/07/81	Van Diemen	Van Diemen RF81-Ford	*Fastest lap*
4	RAC FF1600, round 4	Brands Hatch	12/07/81	Van Diemen	Van Diemen RF81-Ford	*Fastest lap*
1	Townsend-Thoresen FF1600, round 9	Oulton Park	25/07/81	Van Diemen	Van Diemen RF81-Ford	*Fastest lap*
1	RAC FF1600, round 5	Mallory Park	26/07/81	Van Diemen	Van Diemen RF81-Ford	*Fastest lap*
1	Townsend-Thoresen FF1600, round 10	Brands Hatch	02/08/81	Van Diemen	Van Diemen RF81-Ford	
1	RAC FF1600, round 6	Snetterton	09/08/81	Van Diemen	Van Diemen RF81-Ford	*Fastest lap*
1	Townsend-Thoresen FF1600, round 11	Donington Park	15/08/81	Van Diemen	Van Diemen RF81-Ford	
1	Townsend-Thoresen FF1600, round 12	Thruxton	31/08/81	Van Diemen	Van Diemen RF81-Ford	*Pole/Fastest lap*
2	Townsend-Thoresen FF1600, round 13	Brands Hatch	29/09/81	Van Diemen	Van Diemen RF81-Ford	*Fastest lap*

1982

	Race	Circuit	Date	Entrant	Car	Comment
1	Pace British FF2000, round 1	Brands Hatch	07/03/82	Rushen Green Racing	Van Diemen RF82-Ford	*Pole/Fastest lap*
1	Pace British FF2000, round 2	Oulton Park	27/03/82	Rushen Green Racing	Van Diemen RF82-Ford	*Pole/Fastest lap*
1	Pace British FF2000, round 3	Silverstone	28/03/82	Rushen Green Racing	Van Diemen RF82-Ford	*Pole/Fastest lap*
1	Pace British FF2000, round 4	Donington Park	04/04/82	Rushen Green Racing	Van Diemen RF82-Ford	*Pole/Fastest lap*
1	Pace British FF2000, round 5	Snetterton	09/04/82	Rushen Green Racing	Van Diemen RF82-Ford	*Pole/Fastest lap*
1	Pace British FF2000, round 6	Silverstone	12/04/82	Rushen Green Racing	Van Diemen RF82-Ford	*Pole/Fastest lap*
ret	EFDA FF2000, round 1	Zolder	18/04/82	Rushen Green Racing	Van Diemen RF82-Ford	*Engine/Pole*
1	EFDA FF2000, round 2	Donington Park	02/05/82	Rushen Green Racing	Van Diemen RF82-Ford	*Pole/Fastest lap*
1	Pace British FF2000, round 7	Mallory Park	02/05/82	Rushen Green Racing	Van Diemen RF82-Ford	*Fastest lap*
ret	EFDA FF2000, round 3	Zolder	09/05/82	Rushen Green Racing	Van Diemen RF82-Ford	*Spun off/Pole/Fastest lap*
ret	Pace British FF2000, round 8	Oulton Park	30/05/82	Rushen Green Racing	Van Diemen RF82-Ford	*Puncture*
1	Celebrity Race	Oulton Park	30/05/82		Sunbeam Talbot Ti	*Fastest lap*
1	Pace British FF2000, round 9	Brands Hatch	31/05/82	Rushen Green Racing	Van Diemen RF82-Ford	*Fastest lap*
1	Pace British FF2000, round 10	Mallory Park	06/06/82	Rushen Green Racing	Van Diemen RF82-Ford	*Fastest lap*
1	Pace British FF2000, round 11	Brands Hatch	13/06/82	Rushen Green Racing	Van Diemen RF82-Ford	*Fastest lap*
ret	EFDA FF2000, round 4	Hockenheim	20/06/82	Rushen Green Racing	Van Diemen RF82-Ford	*Accident/Pole*
1	Pace British FF2000, round 12	Oulton Park	26/06/82	Rushen Green Racing	Van Diemen RF82-Ford	*Fastest lap*
1	EFDA FF2000, round 5	Zandvoort	03/07/82	Rushen Green Racing	Van Diemen RF82-Ford	*Pole*
2	Pace British FF2000, round 13	Snetterton	04/07/82	Rushen Green Racing	Van Diemen RF82-Ford	
1	Pace British FF2000, round 14	Castle Combe	10/07/82	Rushen Green Racing	Van Diemen RF82-Ford	*Pole/Fastest lap*
1	Pace British FF2000, round 15	Snetterton	01/08/82	Rushen Green Racing	Van Diemen RF82-Ford	*Fastest lap*
1	EFDA FF2000, round 6	Hockenheim	08/08/82	Rushen Green Racing	Van Diemen RF82-Ford	*Pole/Fastest lap*
1	EFDA FF2000, round 7	Osterreichring	15/08/82	Rushen Green Racing	Van Diemen RF82-Ford	*Pole/Fastest lap*
1	EFDA FF2000, round 8	Jyllandsring	22/08/82	Rushen Green Racing	Van Diemen RF82-Ford	*Pole/Fastest lap*
1	Pace British FF2000, round 16	Thruxton	30/08/82	Rushen Green Racing	Van Diemen RF82-Ford	*Fastest lap*
1	Pace British FF2000, round 17	Silverstone	05/09/82	Rushen Green Racing	Van Diemen RF82-Ford	*Fastest lap*
1	EFDA FF2000, round 9	Mondello Park	12/09/82	Rushen Green Racing	Van Diemen RF82-Ford	*Fastest lap*
2	Pace British FF2000, round 20	Brands Hatch	26/09/82	Rushen Green Racing	Van Diemen RF82-Ford	*Fastest lap*
1	Formula 3 Race	Thruxton	13/11/82	West Surrey Racing	Ralt RT3-Toyota	*Pole/Fastest lap*

1983

1	Marlboro British F3, round 1	Silverstone	06/03/83	West Surrey Racing	Ralt RT3-Toyota	*Fastest lap*
1	Marlboro British F3, round 2	Thruxton	13/03/83	West Surrey Racing	Ralt RT3-Toyota	*Pole/Fastest lap*
1	Marlboro British F3, round 3	Silverstone	20/03/83	West Surrey Racing	Ralt RT3-Toyota	*Pole/Fastest lap*
1	Marlboro British F3, round 4	Donington Park	27/03/83	West Surrey Racing	Ralt RT3-Toyota	*Pole/Fastest lap*
1	Marlboro British F3, round 5	Thruxton	04/04/83	West Surrey Racing	Ralt RT3-Toyota	*Pole*
1	Marlboro British F3, round 6	Silverstone	24/04/83	West Surrey Racing	Ralt RT3-Toyota	*Pole/Fastest lap*
1	Marlboro British F3, round 7	Thruxton	02/05/83	West Surrey Racing	Ralt RT3-Toyota	*Pole/Fastest lap*
1	Marlboro British F3, round 8	Brands Hatch	08/05/83	West Surrey Racing	Ralt RT3-Toyota	*Pole/Fastest lap*
1	Marlboro British F3, round 9	Silverstone	30/05/83	West Surrey Racing	Ralt RT3-Toyota	*Pole/Fastest lap*
ret	Marlboro British F3, round 10	Silverstone	12/06/83	West Surrey Racing	Ralt RT3-Toyota	*Crashed at chicane*
dns	Marlboro British F3, round 11	Cadwell Park	19/06/83	West Surrey Racing	Ralt RT3-Toyota	*Crashed in practice/Pole*
ret	Marlboro British F3, round 12	Snetterton	03/07/83	West Surrey Racing	Ralt RT3-Toyota	*Crash with Brundle/Fastest lap*
1	Marlboro British F3, round 13	Silverstone	16/07/83	West Surrey Racing	Ralt RT3-Toyota	*Pole/Fastest lap*
2	Marlboro British F3, round 14	Donington Park	24/07/83	West Surrey Racing	Ralt RT3-Toyota	*Pole/Fastest lap*
ret	Marlboro British F3, round 15	Oulton Park	06/08/83	West Surrey Racing	Ralt RT3-Toyota	*Crash with Brundle/Fastest lap*
1	Marlboro British F3, round 16	Silverstone	29/08/83	West Surrey Racing	Ralt RT3-Toyota	*Pole*
ret	Marlboro British F3, round 17	Oulton Park	11/09/83	West Surrey Racing	Ralt RT3-Toyota	*Crash with Brundle/Pole*
ret	Marlboro British F3, round 18	Thruxton	18/09/83	West Surrey Racing	Ralt RT3-Toyota	*Engine/Pole*
2	Marlboro British F3, round 19	Silverstone	02/10/83	West Surrey Racing	Ralt RT3-Toyota	
1	Macau GP	Macau	20/10/83	Marlboro/Teddy Yip	Ralt RT3-Toyota	*Pole/Fastest lap*
1	Marlboro British F3, round 20	Thruxton	27/10/83	West Surrey Racing	Ralt RT3-Toyota	*Pole/Fastest lap*

1984

ret	BRAZILIAN GP	Rio	25/03/84	Toleman Group Motorsport	Toleman TG183B-Hart	*Turbo boost pressure*
6	SOUTH AFRICAN GP	Kyalami	07/04/84	Toleman Group Motorsport	Toleman TG183B-Hart	*First championship point*
6	BELGIAN GP	Zolder	29/04/84	Toleman Group Motorsport	Toleman TG183B-Hart	*6th place, car disqualified*
dnq	SAN MARINO GP	Imola	06/05/84	Toleman Group Motorsport	Toleman TG183B-Hart	*Tyre/Fuel pump problems*
1	Inaugural Saloon Car Race	Nürburgring	12/05/84	Daimler Benz AG	Mercedes Benz 190E	*First race rebuilt circuit*
ret	FRENCH GP	Dijon	20/05/84	Toleman Group Motorsport	Toleman TG184-Hart	*Turbo*
2	MONACO GP	Monte Carlo	03/07/84	Toleman Group Motorsport	Toleman TG184-Hart	*Race stopped/Fastest lap*
7	CANADIAN GP	Montreal	17/06/84	Toleman Group Motorsport	Toleman TG184-Hart	
ret	DETROIT GP	Detroit	24/06/84	Toleman Group Motorsport	Toleman TG184-Hart	*Broken wishbone/Crashed*
ret	DALLAS GP	Dallas	08/07/84	Toleman Group Motorsport	Toleman TG184-Hart	*Driveshaft*
8	Nürburgring 1000 KMS	Nürburgring	15/07/84	Reinhold Joest Racing Team	Porsche 956	*Pescarolo/Johansson co-drove*
3	BRITISH GP	Brands Hatch	22/07/84	Toleman Group Motorsport	Toleman TG184-Hart	
ret	GERMAN GP	Hockenheim	05/08/84	Toleman Group Motorsport	Toleman TG184-Hart	*Rear wing/Accident*
ret	AUSTRIAN GP	Osterreichring	19/08/84	Toleman Group Motorsport	Toleman TG184-Hart	*Oil pressure*
ret	DUTCH GP	Zandvoort	26/08/84	Toleman Group Motorsport	Toleman TG184-Hart	*Engine*
dns	ITALIAN GP	Monza	09/09/84	Toleman Group Motorsport	Toleman TG184-Hart	*Dropped by team for one race*
ret	EUROPEAN GP	Nürburgring	07/10/84	Toleman Group Motorsport	Toleman TG184-Hart	*Hit Rosberg*
3	PORTUGUESE GP	Estoril	21/10/84	Toleman Group Motorsport	Toleman TG184-Hart	

1985

ret	BRAZILIAN GP	Rio	07/04/85	John Player Team Lotus	Lotus 97T-Renault	*Electrics*
1	PORTUGUESE GP	Estoril	21/04/85	John Player Team Lotus	Lotus 97T-Renault	*Pole/Fastest lap*
7/ret	SAN MARINO GP	Imola	05/05/85	John Player Team Lotus	Lotus 97T-Renault	*Out of fuel/Pole*
ret	MONACO GP	Monte Carlo	19/05/85	John Player Team Lotus	Lotus 97T-Renault	*Engine/Pole*
16	CANADIAN GP	Montreal	16/06/85	John Player Team Lotus	Lotus 97T-Renault	*Pit stop/Fastest lap*
ret	DETROIT GP	Detroit	23/06/85	John Player Team Lotus	Lotus 97T-Renault	*Hit wall/Pole/Fastest lap*
ret	FRENCH GP	Paul Ricard	07/07/85	John Player Team Lotus	Lotus 97T-Renault	*Engine/Accident*
10	BRITISH GP	Silverstone	21/07/85	John Player Team Lotus	Lotus 97T-Renault	*Fuel injection problems*
ret	GERMAN GP	Nürburgring	04/08/85	John Player Team Lotus	Lotus 97T-Renault	*Cv joint*
2	AUSTRIAN GP	Osterreichring	18/08/85	John Player Team Lotus	Lotus 97T-Renault	
3	DUTCH GP	Zandvoort	25/08/85	John Player Team Lotus	Lotus 97T-Renault	
3	ITALIAN GP	Monza	08/09/85	John Player Team Lotus	Lotus 97T-Renault	*Pole*
1	BELGIAN GP	Spa	15/09/85	John Player Team Lotus	Lotus 97T-Renault	
2	EUROPEAN GP	Brands Hatch	06/10/85	John Player Team Lotus	Lotus 97T-Renault	*Pole*
ret	SOUTH AFRICAN GP	Kyalami	19/10/85	John Player Team Lotus	Lotus 97T-Renault	*Engine*
ret	AUSTRALIAN GP	Adelaide	03/11/85	John Player Team Lotus	Lotus 97T-Renault	*Engine/Pole*

1986

2	BRAZILIAN GP	Rio	23/03/86	John Player Team Lotus	Lotus 98T-Renault	*Pole/Incident with Mansell*
1	SPANISH GP	Jerez	13/04/86	John Player Team Lotus	Lotus 98T-Renault	*Pole*
ret	SAN MARINO GP	Imola	27/04/86	John Player Team Lotus	Lotus 98T-Renault	*Wheel bearing/Pole*
3	MONACO GP	Monte Carlo	11/05/86	John Player Team Lotus	Lotus 98T-Renault	
2	BELGIAN GP	Spa	25/05/86	John Player Team Lotus	Lotus 98T-Renault	
5	CANADIAN GP	Montreal	15/06/86	John Player Team Lotus	Lotus 98T-Renault	
1	DETROIT GP	Detroit	22/06/86	John Player Team Lotus	Lotus 98T-Renault	*Pole*
ret	FRENCH GP	Paul Ricard	06/07/86	John Player Team Lotus	Lotus 98T-Renault	*Spun off on oil/Pole*
ret	BRITISH GP	Brands Hatch	13/07/86	John Player Team Lotus	Lotus 98T-Renault	*Gearbox*
2	GERMAN GP	Hockenheim	27/07/86	John Player Team Lotus	Lotus 98T-Renault	
2	HUNGARIAN GP	Hungaroring	10/08/86	John Player Team Lotus	Lotus 98T-Renault	*Pole*
ret	AUSTRIAN GP	Osterreichring	17/08/86	John Player Team Lotus	Lotus 98T-Renault	*Engine*
ret	ITALIAN GP	Monza	07/09/86	John Player Team Lotus	Lotus 98T-Renault	*Transmission*
4	PORTUGUESE GP	Estoril	21/09/86	John Player Team Lotus	Lotus 98T-Renault	*Pole*
3	MEXICAN GP	Mexico City	12/10/86	John Player Team Lotus	Lotus 98T-Renault	*Pole*
ret	AUSTRALIAN GP	Adelaide	26/10/86	John Player Team Lotus	Lotus 98T-Renault	*Engine*

1987

ret	BRAZILIAN GP	Rio	12/04/87	Camel Team Lotus Honda	Lotus 99T-Honda	*Engine*
2	SAN MARINO GP	Imola	03/05/87	Camel Team Lotus Honda	Lotus 99T-Honda	*Pole*
ret	BELGIAN GP	Spa	17/05/87	Camel Team Lotus Honda	Lotus 99T-Honda	*Accident with Mansell*
1	MONACO GP	Monte Carlo	31/05/87	Camel Team Lotus Honda	Lotus 99T-Honda	*Fastest lap*
1	DETROIT GP	Detroit	21/06/87	Camel Team Lotus Honda	Lotus 99T-Honda	*Fastest lap*
4	FRENCH GP	Paul Ricard	05/07/87	Camel Team Lotus Honda	Lotus 99T-Honda	
3	BRITISH GP	Silverstone	12/07/87	Camel Team Lotus Honda	Lotus 99T-Honda	
3	GERMAN GP	Hockenheim	26/07/87	Camel Team Lotus Honda	Lotus 99T-Honda	
2	HUNGARIAN GP	Hungaroring	09/08/87	Camel Team Lotus Honda	Lotus 99T-Honda	
5	AUSTRIAN GP	Osterreichring	16/08/87	Camel Team Lotus Honda	Lotus 99T-Honda	
2	ITALIAN GP	Monza	06/09/87	Camel Team Lotus Honda	Lotus 99T-Honda	*Fastest lap*
7	PORTUGUESE GP	Estoril	20/09/87	Camel Team Lotus Honda	Lotus 99T-Honda	*Pit stop/Throttle problems*
5	SPANISH GP	Jerez	27/09/87	Camel Team Lotus Honda	Lotus 99T-Honda	*Tyre problems*
ret	MEXICAN GP	Mexico City	18/10/87	Camel Team Lotus Honda	Lotus 99T-Honda	*Spun off*
2	JAPANESE GP	Suzuka	01/11/87	Camel Team Lotus Honda	Lotus 99T-Honda	
dsq	AUSTRALIAN GP	Adelaide	15/11/87	Camel Team Lotus Honda	Lotus 99T-Honda	*Oversize brake ducts*

1988

dsq	BRAZILIAN GP	Rio	03/04/88	Honda Marlboro McLaren	McLaren MP4/4-Honda	*Changed cars illegally/Pole*
1	SAN MARINO GP	Imola	01/05/88	Honda Marlboro McLaren	McLaren MP4/4-Honda	*Pole*
ret	MONACO GP	Monte Carlo	15/05/88	Honda Marlboro McLaren	McLaren MP4/4-Honda	*Hit barrier/Pole/Fastest lap*
2	MEXICAN GP	Mexico City	29/05/88	Honda Marlboro McLaren	McLaren MP4/4-Honda	*Pole*
1	CANADIAN GP	Montreal	12/06/88	Honda Marlboro McLaren	McLaren MP4/4-Honda	*Pole/Fastest lap*
1	DETROIT GP	Detroit	19/06/88	Honda Marlboro McLaren	McLaren MP4/4-Honda	*Pole*
2	FRENCH GP	Paul Ricard	03/07/88	Honda Marlboro McLaren	McLaren MP4/4-Honda	
1	BRITISH GP	Silverstone	10/07/88	Honda Marlboro McLaren	McLaren MP4/4-Honda	
1	GERMAN GP	Hockenheim	24/07/88	Honda Marlboro McLaren	McLaren MP4/4-Honda	*Pole*
1	HUNGARIAN GP	Hungaroring	08/08/88	Honda Marlboro McLaren	McLaren MP4/4-Honda	*Pole*
1	BELGIAN GP	Spa	28/08/88	Honda Marlboro McLaren	McLaren MP4/4-Honda	*Pole*
ret	ITALIAN GP	Monza	11/09/88	Honda Marlboro McLaren	McLaren MP4/4-Honda	*Accident with Schlesser/Pole*
6	PORTUGUESE GP	Estoril	25/09/88	Honda Marlboro McLaren	McLaren MP4/4-Honda	*Hit by Mansell/Pit stop*
4	SPANISH GP	Jerez	02/10/88	Honda Marlboro McLaren	McLaren MP4/4-Honda	*Pit stop/Pole*
1	JAPANESE GP	Suzuka	30/10/88	Honda Marlboro McLaren	McLaren MP4/4-Honda	*Delayed at start/Pole/Fastest lap*
2	AUSTRALIAN GP	Adelaide	13/11/88	Honda Marlboro McLaren	McLaren MP4/4-Honda	*Pole*

Kart World Championship positions

1977	6th
1979	2nd
1980	2nd
1981	4th

Kart Championship wins

1977 South American Championship
1978 South American Championship
1978 Brazilian Championship
1979 Brazilian Championship
1980 Brazilian Championship
1981 Brazilian Championship

Formula 1 World Championship positions

1984	9th=
1985	4th
1986	4th
1987	3rd
1988	1st

Other Motor Racing Championship wins

1981 RAC FF1600 Champion
1981 Townsend-Thoresen FF1600 Champion
1982 Pace British FF2000 Champion
1982 EFDA FF2000 Champion
1983 Marlboro British F3 Champion